Here's How

Be a Super Sitter

DR. LEE SALK
JAY LITVIN

NTC LEARNINGWORKS
NTC/Contemporary Publishing Company

Parents: Please read

The information provided in the Super Sitters printed material is primarily intended for prevention of physical, psychological, and emotional injury to children while under the supervision of a babysitter. The child care and first aid procedures contained in the material do not take the place of a certified course in first aid, CPR, child care or babysitting. Review of this material by a babysitter does not constitute certification or competency in babysitting, child care, first aid or CPR. Parents maintain sole responsibility for the competency of the sitters they hire for the care of their children. We urge parents to select their sitters carefully and if possible to obtain sitters who have received babysitting, child care, first aid, and CPR training from a qualified source.

While the procedures and suggestions contained within the Super Sitters' materials are within approved medical and pediatric practice (1988), all parents have different ways of responding to their children. Before leaving their children in the care of a sitter, parents should review carefully all the Super Sitters material and indicate to their sitters any areas where they may find a discrepancy between the way they want their children cared for and any child care method suggested in the Super Sitters material.

Library of Congress Cataloging-in-Publication Data

Litvin, Jay, 1944–
        [How to be a super sitter]
        Be a super sitter / Lee Salk and Jay Litvin.
            p.   cm.—(Here's how)
        Originally published: How to be a super sitter / Jay Litvin, Lee Salk. © 1991.
        Summary: Gives advice to young babysitters on getting jobs, keeping a business going, and safe handling of babies and children.
        ISBN 0-8442-2481-2
        1. Babysitting—Handbooks, manuals, etc.—Juvenile literature.
[1. Babysitting.]   I. Salk, Lee, 1926–   .   II. Title.
III. Series
HQ769.5.L58   1997
649'.1'0248—dc21   97-46104
                                                CIP

Cover illustrations by Art Glazer

Published by NTC LearningWorks
An imprint of NTC/Contemporary Publishing Company
4255 West Touhy Avenue, Lincolnwood (Chicago), Illinois 60646-1975 U.S.A.
Copyright © 1998 by Super Sitters, Inc.
Printed in the United States of America
International Standard Book Number: 0-8442-2481-2

18   17   16   15   14   13   12   11   10   9   8   7   6   5   4   3   2   1

Contents

Acknowledgments

We wish to acknowledge the following individuals and organizations for their consultation, information and support:

Edwin Montgomery, Jr., M.D., Fellow of the American Academy of Pediatrics
Dennis Maiman, M.D., Ph.D.
William Braunstein, M.D.
John Rubinow, M.D.
Evangeline M. Vukmir, R.N., M.S., Certified Pediatric Nurse Practitioner
Michael Scahill, R.N., B.S.N., Certified Pediatric Nurse Practitioner
Becky Doman, EMT, Menomonee Falls (Wisconsin) Fire Department
Dennis Schulteis, EMT, Menomonee Falls (Wisconsin) Fire Department
National Association of Pediatric Nurse and Associate Practitioners
Sharon Litvin
Harry, Allen and Max Samson
Mark Koerner
Sherry Levin
Hanson Graphic
Tim Fuller Photography

Thanks to Phil Orkin for researching and editing material for this handbook.

About the Authors

Dr. Lee Salk is one of America's foremost authorities on child development. He is clinical professor of psychology in psychiatry and clinical professor of pediatrics at the New York Hospital—Cornell Medical Center. Dr. Salk is consulting editor of *Baby Talk Magazine* and a monthly contributor to *McCalls*. A frequent guest on national radio and TV programs, Dr. Salk is also the author of many books, including *Your Child's First Year, The Complete Dr. Salk* and *Preparing for Parenthood.*

Jay Litvin, a resident of Milwaukee, Wisconsin, and father of six, created the Super Sitters concept from both his personal and professional experience. An accomplished film producer with an education degree in personal growth and development, Litvin has helped develop and film critically acclaimed documentaries for public television and private industry. His credits include positions as corporate head of communications for a large health care company and clinical director of a respected mental health clinic in Tucson, Arizona.

Introduction

Babysitting. It's a great way to gain extra cash, but it's also much more than that.

Sitting is rewarding. It's a service that lets you do something for others and gives you a unique chance to have a positive effect on younger kids.

Sitting is also a business. In fact, it might be your first "real" job. Babysitting can give you the experience you'll need to land other jobs in the future. You'll learn how to schedule your time, how to go on job interviews, how to find clients and keep them happy. You'll build up confidence in yourself—confidence you'll carry with you for the rest of your life.

Babysitting opportunities have never been better. Today there are more families than ever before with both parents working outside the home, and many families with just one parent running the household. Today's parents have a variety of child care needs, and babysitting is usually one of them. Most parents are eager (even desperate!) to hire quality sitters for their children, and they're willing to pay top dollar for sitters they know they can trust.

Parents have a right to expect quality care for their children, whether it's in day-care centers or with babysitters. By following the methods in this workbook, you can become the kind of sitter parents dream of.

Of course, there are real challenges and responsibilities that come with the good opportunities of today. Good babysitting is *not* talking on the phone, watching TV, or doing homework instead of actively caring for the kids. And it isn't just changing diapers, wiping runny noses, and playing games.

You'll need to be safe, conscientious, and caring. You'll have to be honest and professional. And you'll have to be willing to follow the rules parents have for their families, even if they're different from the ones you're used to.

How to Be a Super Sitter is a great tool to help you start your own babysitting business. By going through its pages, you'll find out if sitting is right for you. If it is, we'll show you where to begin. We explain where to get training, how to get those first clients, and how to properly take care of infants, toddlers, and older children. You'll find out how to have fun with the kids you look after, and you'll learn how to handle first aid and emergency situations.

You'll also learn how to cooperate with parents, how to keep track of your business and your time. You'll find forms and charts to keep you organized and out of trouble. And you'll learn to be a positive influence on children.

So, if you're ready, let's find out if you've got what it takes to be a Super Sitter!

1

Is Super Sitting For Me?

While babysitting may seem like a simple job to do, it's really not for everyone. Most young people can learn the basic skills needed for safe, fun sitting, but not everyone has the interest, enthusiasm, and personality to care for children.

Before you decide to start up a sitting business, let's make sure you're cut out for the job.

Checklist #1

Ask yourself the following questions and put check marks in the appropriate spaces. Be sure to answer honestly.

YES	NO	
☑	☐	Do I really like young children?
☑	☐	Am I an honest person?
☑	☐	Am I naturally friendly?
☑	☐	Can I be nice, but firm if I have to?
☑	☐	Do I have basic common sense?
☑	☐	Am I a patient person?
☑	☑	Do I have a lot of energy?
☑	☒	Can I be sensitive to children's needs?
☑	☐	Can I respect the privacy of others?
☑	☐	Can I respect the property of others?

If you answered "yes" to all of the above questions, you're definitely Super Sitters material. If you answer "no" to any, think about how you can change those no's to yes's. If you don't think you can, babysitting is probably not the best job for you.

It's one thing to be an honest, caring person who likes kids, but it takes even more to be a good sitter. The following checklist gives you an idea of what we mean.

 *Checklist #2*

Answer the following honestly by putting a check in the appropriate column.

YES   NO

☑ ☐ Do you feel kids are funny and creative?

☑ ☐ Could you cheerfully change a messy diaper?

☑ ☐ Could you help a toddler get on and off the toilet?

☑ ☐ Can you take 20 minutes of nonstop crying without losing your patience?

☑ ☐ Can you stay positive and friendly through hours of spilled drinks, skinned knees, and temper tantrums.

If you answered "yes" to these questions, you're on your way to a satisfying sitting career. A "no" answer to any of the above may mean that you need to spend more time around young children before babysitting, or maybe sitting just isn't for you.

Do I Have the Time to Be a Super Sitter?

When you're starting a babysitting business, you have to be realistic about certain things. One of the most important things to think about is how much time you have available to babysit. Are you involved in after-school activities like sports or music? Does your family have rules about being out on school nights? Will any of these things hinder your ability to be a reliable sitter?

If you're starting your business during the summer months, what are your family's vacation plans? Are there activities that you want to be part of during the summer?

List all of the activities you have during the week. Include study time, family time, and time with friends.

I go to hawaiian falls alot
I am going to Kansees in
the ~~summer~~ August
weekends sleepovers

After doing this, ask yourself, "Is starting a sitting business a realistic project?" During the school year, parents need sitters in the evening and on weekends. During the summer, some parents need sitters every day while they are at work. How much time can you give?

Let's Get Busy! Let's Get Experience.

You've completed chapter 1, and you're now convinced you want to be a Super Sitter. The next question is: "Do I have enough experience caring for children to start right in? Or, do I need to get some basic training before I get my first babysitting job?"

Have you cared for younger brothers or sisters? Have you watched your little nieces or nephews? Do you know how to change a diaper or give a baby a bottle? Have you handled a toddler who is being potty trained? Have you survived the temper tantrums of a two-year-old? Do you know how to make an emergency phone call to the police or ambulance? Do you know the basics of first aid?

Ways to Get Basic Experience

If you've had a lot of experience in the areas just described, you can skip this section and go on to chapter 3. If you really don't feel confident about tackling that first sitting assignment, don't worry; here's where to get experience you need to be a Super Sitter.

In the Family

By offering to care for your younger brothers and sisters, you can gain valuable experience in sitting. Maybe you have an older brother or sister who has young children. Will an aunt or uncle let you come over and read a bedtime story to your niece or nephew? It's easier to ask relatives how they do things like bathe an infant or diaper a toddler, and maybe they can use the extra help.

Make a list of family members to contact for help in gaining hands-on sitter experience:

Name	Relationship	Phone Number
Michael T	Dad	913-3146216
Lizz T	mom	913-972-8558
Carol T	grandma	
Norman T	grandpa	

Friends and Neighbors

If asking family members isn't a good idea, try asking some friends or neighbors who know you. Explain that you want to become a good sitter and that you'd like to look after their little ones under their supervision. It may be easier to start with children who know you already.

List possible neighbors and friends to ask:

Name	Address	Phone Number
Skylar	unknown	?
Syndey	wild poar	?
Emerson	?	?

If you ask friends to help you gain some experience, start out with a job you can handle. Don't try caring for twin infants! Start with a child you know and sit for a short period of time. Gaining experience slowly but surely is the best way. Don't be afraid to ask questions.

Experienced Sitters

You can always gain from someone else's babysitting experience. Ask an older brother or sister, or a friend or relative to give you some advice. Ask an experienced sitter if you can come along on one of their jobs as a nonpaid helper. Then you can watch how an experienced sitter does things (make sure the other sitter has permission from the family).

List some experienced sitters you could ask for help:

Name	Address	Phone Number
old sitter 1	?	?
old sitter2	?	?
old sitter3	?	?
old sitter4	?	?
		?

Team Up with a Friend

A partnership with a good friend may help you face the challenge of gaining sitting experience. It's fun to go through a Red Cross babysitting course or a first aid course with someone who also wants to learn to be a Super Sitter.

Volunteer Your Services

Look for places where you can volunteer and gain child care experience. Perhaps your church or temple has a child care service, or maybe there are programs for younger kids at your local YMCA or community center. Preschools and day-care centers in your neighborhood may be other good places to check out. By offering your services for free, you'll be able to work with children under supervision. You may also meet children and parents who could become future clients for your business.

List local organizations to contact about volunteering your time. Use the phone book to look up phone numbers and addresses:

Name	Address	Phone Number
_____	_____	_____
_____	_____	_____
_____	_____	_____
_____	_____	_____
_____	_____	_____
_____	_____	_____
_____	_____	_____
_____	_____	_____

Take Classes and Courses

Schools often offer babysitting classes. The local Red Cross, police and fire stations, YWCA's, libraries, or medical clinics may also have programs designed to train sitters. Contact your local 4H Club or Girl Scout troop, too. Find out if you can participate in one of these programs. You'll feel more confident about striking out on your own. In addition, Super Sitters, Inc., has a complete home training program for sitters. Check the list of additional resources in the back of this workbook for more information.

List training programs offered in your area:

Name	Address	Phone Number
_____	_____	_____
	_____	
_____	_____	_____
	_____	

_____   _____   _____

_____

_____   _____   _____

_____

Once you've completed the lists in this chapter, you may want to set some goals for yourself. For example, in addition to using this workbook as a guide, you may decide to take a Red Cross course and practice sitting for your little sister during the next month—before starting your sitting business. Or you may volunteer at your church day-care center and take a CPR course at your local firehouse. Whatever you do, write down your plan below, and stick to it until you've accomplished your goals.

Use the following space to list the goals you need to reach in order to have enough experience to start your Super Sitters business:

1. Complete the "How to Be A Super Sitter" handbook

2. do CPR

3. Call for help

4. make the child calm

5. Stay calm

6. wait till help arrives

7.

8.

9.

10.

_____

_____

_____

_____

_____

_____

_____

_____

_____

_____

_____

_____

_____

_____

_____

_____

_____

_____

_____

_____

_____

_____

_____

Setting Up Your Business

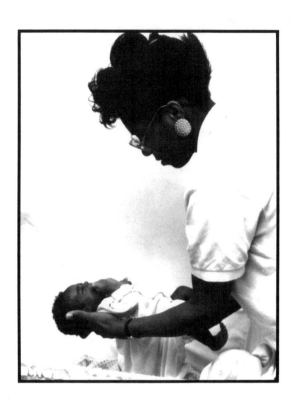

What Do I Charge?

Babysitters are paid different amounts in every part of the country. The hourly rate in Appleton, Wisconsin, is not the same as in New York City. People pay their sitters what they can afford. They try to take into account things like experience, age, and reputation of the sitter.

What Does My Competition Charge?

The first thing to do is find out what your competition is charging. Ask friends and neighbors what they pay for a very good sitter. What do they pay for a relatively inexperienced sitter? You need to know this information so that you don't overcharge customers or undersell your talents. Don't be greedy. If the best sitters in your area charge $2.00 per hour, and you're just starting, ask for the minimum until your experience and reputation grow.

Rates Can Change with Time of Day

Some parents will pay more during daylight hours than at night because their children will be awake and need more attention. Some sitters charge more past midnight.

Consistency Counts

Once you decide on your rates, stick to them. Charge the same rates to everyone within a given area. If you play favorites with some families by charging less, your others clients may hear about it and feel that you're cheating them. Being consistent helps keep your good reputation from being tarnished.

One more thing: when you change your rate, change your rate for everyone, and let all of your customers know at the same time.

Are You Sitting for More than One Child?

If you're going to sit for more than one child at a time, you may want to adjust your rate. For example, if you charge $1.75 per hour for one child, you might charge $2.00 or $2.25 for two, or $2.50 per hour for three. See what other sitters are charging in this situation. There is no set rule about this, and it's best to follow common practice.

Do I Charge Extra for Cleaning Up?

Never charge extra for cleaning up a mess you and the kids create while babysitting. But, if a parent asks you to do extra cleaning, like washing the dinner dishes or vacuuming the living room rug, you can ask for an extra fee. Cleaning up a mess you didn't create is *not* part of babysitting. Those dishes might cost an extra $1.00, for example. Talk it over with the parents *before* you sit. As long as such things are clearly stated ahead of time, there won't be hard feelings between you and parents.

Your Sitting Business and Taxes

The Internal Revenue Service requires that sitters who make over a certain amount per year pay federal income tax. Super Sitters encourages sitters and parents to contact their local state and federal tax offices for the most current information on babysitting and taxes.

Managing Your Time

If you can, purchase a calendar or pocket appointment book to keep track of all of your activities, including babysitting jobs. As we mentioned earlier, it is important not to overextend yourself when time is concerned. To help you get started on properly managing your time, we suggest you copy the calendar blank on the next page and fill in your nonbabysitting activities for the next two months. As things come up, fill in the calendar.

Sun	Mon	Tues	Wed	Thur	Fri	Sat

The Dangers of Overscheduling

By using the calendar, you can keep from overscheduling yourself. Overscheduling will lead to your forgetting babysitting jobs or having to cancel at the last moment because of other commitments. The easiest way to lose customers is to cancel at the last moment. Keeping track of your calendars will allow you to balance school, free time and Super Sitting. You'll be surprised at how much more you can accomplish by keeping track of all of your activities.

Invoices and Receipts

Some parents will want to deduct the money they pay you from their income tax. While you really don't have to give your customers receipts when you sit for them, it will help them for tax purposes and will give your business a professional look. You may want to purchase a simple receipt book at a nearby office supply store. Or, maybe you'd like to use the following format as a guide:

Jane Smith 1515 N. Main Street Any Town, WI 53000 414/555-5555			**Receipt** Number: 001 Date:
Charge to: <u>Customer Name</u>			

Description	# of Hours	$/Hour	Total
Babysat for Johnny & Mary	3	$2.25/hr.	$6.75
		Total	$6.75

4

Building Your Business

Experts say that every new business is like a three-legged stool. The first leg is the product or service. It has to be good or people will not use it. The second leg is good financial recordkeeping. Recordkeeping lets you know whether it's really worth being in business and helps you pay your fair share of taxes. Businesses without good bookkeeping usually don't last very long. The third leg is good advertising and marketing. These are ways of letting people know who you are and what services you have to offer. Without this leg, you can be the best sitter in the world and keep the best records in the world and still go out of business because no one will know you're available and reliable. Like the three-legged stool, if any one of these legs in a business is missing, there's a good chance the business is in for a tumble.

Here are some tips on how to get those first babysitting jobs:

Word of Mouth

This is the simplest and most common way of getting sitting jobs. You start out by working for family, neighbors, and friends. If you do the best job possible for these first clients, you'll start to build a good reputation. Let your satisfied customers know that you are available for other sitting jobs, so that when one of *their* friends or relatives is in need of a sitter, they'll recommend you for the job. The best advertisement for a Super Sitter is satisfied clients. Don't be afraid to ask the parents you sit for to pass the word along that you are a reliable, available sitter.

Notice Boards

Many food stores, community centers, churches, synagogues, and apartment buildings in your area have public bulletin boards. You can create a brief, clearly written notice that lets people know about your sitting business. Your notice should have pull-off slips with your phone number. To be on the safe side, don't put your name or address on the notice. Your phone number is enough. You need to be aware of the rare person who might misuse too much information about you. Always check with the store to find out their posting rules, and follow them carefully.

Here's a possible format for a notice:

```
Safe, Reliable Babysitter Available

for Weekday Evenings and Weekends

Infants * Toddlers * Older Children

References Available - Reasonable Rates
```

phone #	phone #	phone #	phone #	phone #	phone #	phone #	phone #	phone #	phone #	phone #	phone #

If you take a babysitting or first aid class, mention that on the notice too. Let your parents know you are expecting people to call about hiring you. Be prepared to give callers the names and phone numbers of satisfied customers for them to call as references.

Classified Ads

A small inexpensive ad in your weekly community newspaper or shopper can help you get more business. Call the publication you want to advertise in and ask about their rates before placing an ad.

Here's a sample of a possible ad:

Need A
Babysitter?

Call:
555-5555

Safe, Reliable
Care for Infants
Toddlers &
Older Kids

Available
Weekday Evenings
and Weekends

References Available

Local papers and shopping flyers will usually help you write a classified ad. They will charge you for the ad space but offer their help for free.

Some Other Strategies

Some communities have teen employment services. They can list your business and pass your phone number along to parents who call them looking for sitters. Check with your school system, town council, or chamber of commerce to see what services are available to you. Another idea is to leave flyers or notices at local day-care centers. Ask the day-care directors for permission before advertising your services.

Have a Plan

As it is with everything else, it's easier to get things done if you have a written plan to follow. Use the sample below as a guide to set goals, plan your marketing and advertising activities, and follow through.

Date you will start project	Description of Marketing or Advertising Project	Date Project Completed
Sept. 1	Call my best customers and ask them to let their family and friends know that I am available for other sitting jobs. Ask them if I can use their names and phone numbers for references with new customers.	Sept. 1
Sept. 4	1. Go to the ten busiest stores that have bulletin boards. Ask managers if I can post a notice.	Sept. 4
Sept. 5	2. Make up 10 notices for local bulletin boards. Distribute them.	Sept. 5
Sept. 6	1. Call the free shopping flyers in the area and our weekly newspaper to find out how much they charge for a small classified ad. Discuss prices with parents.	Sept. 6
Sept. 6	2. Write ad and either call it in to the newspaper(s) or deliver it.	Sept. 7

5

Choosing Your Jobs

As you gain in experience and reputation, new customers will come your way. It is important that you thoroughly check out every new family before accepting a job.

Phone Screening

Chances are your first contact with a potential new customer will come over the phone. Use this first conversation to find out if you really want to work for this person. Have a list of questions ready (see Checklist #4 for good questions to ask).

Present Yourself as a Professional

Parents usually have many questions for a new sitter. The following checklist gives you an idea of what information you'll need to give:

☑ **Checklist #3**

☑ How long have you been a sitter?

☑ What ages are you comfortable sitting for?

☑ When are you available?

☑ What do you charge?

☒ Have you ever had to handle an emergency?

☒ Do you have a list of references?

Here is a list of questions for you to ask potential customers:

☑ **Checklist #4**

☑ How did they hear about your babysitting business?

☑ How many children would you be caring for?

☑ What ages are the children?

☑ What part of town do they live in?

☒ Will they be able to provide transportation if necessary? Will they drive you home?

☑ Are your rates acceptable?

☒ Do these children have special needs (are they disabled, ill)?

Be friendly and polite, but be firm about things that are important to you. Let them know that you have to be home on time following a job. Be honest about things you aren't comfortable doing. If you don't feel confident about bathing an infant, or preparing food, let them know now. It may cost you a job, but you won't be putting yourself in situations you can't handle.

If the conversation goes well, ask if you can come over to meet the children before accepting the job. This way you'll see if you and the kids will get along, and you'll see the home before saying yes or no. Unless you know the potential customers, or they have been referred by someone you know well, it's a good idea to have a parent come along. You may even want to have a parent speak to them over the phone first. If someone you know referred them to you, call that person and get some information about your potential new customer.

When a New Customer is a Stranger

If your potential customer was not referred to you by a friend or relative, be cautious. Insist on an in-person interview at the customer's home and bring a parent along. A face-to-face meeting will allow you and your parent to decide if this is a proper job to accept. If you have any doubts at all after this meeting, turn the job down. If you feel scared or uncomfortable, trust your feelings. There will be plenty of other good opportunities.

6

Getting Ready for the Job!

Congratulations! If you followed all of the steps presented previously, you've been hired for your first sitting job. You've started your Super Sitters business, and you're in for a lot of rewarding fun. But remember, you're now going to be responsible for the life of a child. During the time you babysit, the children will rely on you for all of their needs. Physical safety and security are primary, but children have other needs as well: friendship, companionship, understanding, and patience.

You're very important to the children. While you're there to keep them safe, you also become part of their growing up. The time you spend with them can have a lasting effect on the rest of their lives.

Children are sensitive. They respond to how they are treated. They watch and listen to everything you do. Make sure to listen when they talk to you. Show that you can be trusted. Be nice. Be fair. In their own ways, the children you care for will be very aware of these things about you. By listening to them, paying attention to them, and treating them gently and fairly, you can help them grow up to be kind and fair people who feel good about themselves and about others.

A Super Sitter believes babysitting is special time, not just killing time. A Super Sitter takes an active part in a child's life: playing, talking, and taking a genuine interest in the child.

The information in the remainder of this handbook will provide you with the information you'll need to develop the knowledge and skills of a Super Sitter. You'll learn medical and emergency procedures. You'll learn about children of different ages. You'll get ideas for activities. And you'll see how to avoid some of the pitfalls that often accompany child care.

You'll learn how to manage mealtime, bath time, and bedtime. We'll guide you through temper tantrums and crying infants. We'll let you know what information you should have about the children in your care, their parents, and their house.

Super Sitter Forms

On pages 62–75 you'll find some forms that will help you gather important information about the children you care for, their parents, and their home. These include:

1 Child's Personal Profile: This form will help you keep track of information about the child's special little habits, routines, and house rules. Does the child use a pacifier? What should you do if the child wakes up during the night? What does the child eat? What comforts the child if he or she is scared or lonely? The forms in the Child's Personal Profile will help you answer these questions.

2 Medical Release Form: You must have this form in case you have to take the child to the doctor or hospital. (This form is on page 117.)

3 Location of Household Items: This form will answer questions like: Where's the broom? The first aid kit? The flashlight? Fuses?

4 Emergency Phone Numbers: You should have numbers for these people: doctor, police, poison control, next-door neighbor (or other neighbor you may contact in case of emergency), grandparents.

Turn to pages 62–75 and familiarize yourself with the forms. You may want to copy a set for each of your customers. Fill them out in pencil when you first start sitting. In an emergency, you'll want to know where they are without having to search for them. Copies of these forms are available from Super Sitters, Inc., by writing to the address listed in the back of this handbook.

Things You Need to Know

Take responsibility for getting the information you need. Parents will appreciate the fact that you care enough about their child to insist on details. The forms on pages 62–75 will make this easier.

Appearance: How Should You Look?

Always look neat and clean. Wear attractive clothing, but not your best. Wear comfortable clothes that will let you play on the floor with the child you're babysitting. Be prepared for the weather. In winter, an extra sweater might come in handy if the house where you're sitting is kept on the cool side. If you plan to play outside with the children, dress appropriately. Don't wear jewelry that might attract the hands of a small child. Leave your pointy rings and dangling earrings at home—kids love to grab and pull.

The First Visit

Arrange to arrive a bit early for your first visit with a family. Ask if you can come over 15 or 20 minutes early. This will give you time to get acquainted with the child (or children) before the parents rush off. You'll also have time to get certain important information from the parents. Ask for a quick tour of the home so you can find bathrooms, light switches, and bedrooms. This is a good time to fill out a set of Super Sitters forms.

Information You Need to Know

About the Parents

 *Checklist #5*

Emergency Numbers

☒ Get numbers for fire, police, rescue, doctor, neighbors, and grandparents.

☑ Know the address and phone number of the house where you're sitting.

Where Are They Going?

☑ Get the name, address, and telephone number.

☑ Find out what time they expect to get there and when they expect to leave. If the parents are going to more than one place, get the approximate time they will change locations.

☐ Get the row and seat numbers of their theater or concert tickets.

Are they going to a restaurant? Find out the name used for their reservation—it will make it easier to locate them in a hurry.

☐ What time do they expect to return home?

☐ Do they expect any phone calls or visitors? Who? How can you identify the visitors—and should you let them in? What do the parents want you to say?

About the Child

Checklist #6:

Meals and Menus

☐ When is mealtime? What's the menu?

☐ May the child have a snack? When? Ask for snack suggestions.

☐ Ask what you may eat, and stick to what you're offered.

Medication

☐ Do not give the child any medications unless instructed by the parents. Have them write down the name of the medication, the correct dosage, and what time it should be given to the child. Ask for helpful hints to get the medicine down successfully. Be sure the medication is out of the child's reach.

Playtime

☐ Are there special play areas inside the house? Are the children allowed to play outside?

☐ Are playmates allowed in the yard? Are they allowed in the house? Is the child allowed to go to a friend's house? Which friend may the child visit? What are the friend's address and telephone number?

Bedtime

☐ When is bedtime? Have there been any recent problems going to bed? Is there a favorite story or bedtime friend? Does the child use a pacifier or security blanket?

About the House

✔ *Checklist #7*

Locks, Alarms, and Extra Keys

☐ Where are they? How do they work? How do the windows work? Is there a security system?

Emergency Supplies

☐ Check the Super Sitters' Location of Household Items on page 74, and make sure it's complete. Ask about flashlights, candles and matches, first aid and cleaning supplies.

Appliances

☐ Be sure you know how to work the can opener, stove, microwave, high chair, infant swing, and anything else you may need to use during the time you're sitting.

Pets

☐ If pets come with the job, do they need to be fed? When, what, and how much should they be fed? Are you supposed to let them outside?

Safety First

Your first concern for the children should always be their safety.

Routine Safety Concerns

Checklist #8

Watch for these common safety problems:

☐ Don't allow a baby or toddler out of your sight unless he or she is safely confined to a crib or playpen.

☐ Never leave a baby unattended on a changing table, in a high chair, or in a bath. Use safety straps if they're available.

☐ Never hold a baby while handling hot foods or drinks, or while cooking or doing dishes.

☐ Because they are allowed to do more things and experiment more freely, older children are actually exposed to many more serious dangers. Stay close enough to step in quickly.

☐ Never open the door to a stranger.

☐ Find out where dangerous cleaners, insect sprays, medicines, and other hazards are kept.

Super Sitters Tip . . . .

Crawling babies find trouble. Get down on the floor with the baby and look for dangerous and tempting things like cords, electrical outlets, knickknacks, nutshells and candy dishes, tabletops with sharp corners, and lamps that might fall. Never let a baby crawl out of sight.

Other Hazards

Be on the lookout for these things:

☑ *Checklist #9*

☐ Small objects that could be swallowed, including carrots, hard candies, and all nuts, which can cause a baby to choke;

☐ clutter that could cause a fall;

☐ stairs;

☐ toys that are safe for older children but unsafe for young children and babies;

☐ open and unscreened windows and doors, uncovered and empty electrical outlets, cords, fans, fireplaces, smoking materials, and tools.

Rules of the Road

The Big No's:

No drinking   **No visitors**
No drugs   **No arriving late**
No smoking

1 Ask the parents if it's all right to watch TV with the children, and find out which programs are allowed. Don't ignore the children because of the TV. Involved, active play is a Super Sitter's job.

2 Stay off the telephone. You can't play with the children while you're chatting with a friend. Parents want to reach you when they call home.

3 Don't snoop. Use only things necessary to care for the child. Respect the family's privacy.

4 No sleeping on the job. You must be able to hear a baby whimpering, a child calling, or a prowler prowling.

5 If the parents leave food for you, don't overdo it. Be sure to leave the kitchen at least as clean as you found it.

6 Give parents a complete report. Tell them about the child's behavior, any problems, phone messages, injuries, broken items.

7 Get an escort home.

Never let a drunk or drugged parent drive you home. If necessary, call your own parents to come and get you. They won't mind being awakened when your safety is at stake.

> *Tell your parents immediately if a parent acts inappropriately with you. And don't babysit there again.*

Super Sitters **Tip** ·

Put a card in your wallet with your own name, address, telephone number, and the name and telephone number of your own doctor. Include your parents' telephone numbers at work. Be ready for your own emergency needs, too.

Meeting the Children

Don't Expect to Be Instant Friends

Build the child's confidence in you by showing concern and understanding. Demonstrate that you are a nice person and that you and the child will have fun together. Ask the child to show you his or her toys or special stuffed animal. Sometimes it helps to bring a Super Sitters Fun Bag of special activities. See page 58 of this handbook for ideas for your Fun Bag.

Separation Anxiety

Some children get upset when the sitter arrives because they know that your arrival means their parents will be leaving. This behavior is normal and, after a short period of sadness, the child will usually respond positively to you. In the meantime, assure the child that his or her parents will come home, and attempt to find an interesting activity for both of you to do.

Disabled Children Have Special Needs

Most likely you will not be asked to care for a child who is severely mentally or physically disabled. However, there are many children with mild disabilities that require only a little extra concern and attention. In this case the parents will probably give you detailed instructions about the special needs of their children. If not, ask them exactly what to do. While there are many things to find out about children with special needs, here are some of the basics:

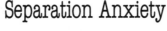 *Checklist #10*

☐ What kind of special help does the disabled child need?

☐ Are there any things the child should not do?

☐ Are there any activities that are especially enjoyable for the child?

☐ Are there any communication problems you might encounter because of the child's difficulty with speaking, hearing, understanding, or ability to follow instructions?

Children with special needs are generally very special little people who are deserving of your very special attention. Give it to them. They're worth it.

Behavior and Discipline

Your job is to make sitting a pleasant experience for the child. The key to successful behavior management is to establish a good relationship with the child from the beginning. Every child is unique, and each child responds differently to problem situations and to different methods of behavior management. Take the time to get to know the child.

Most children misbehave at times. Remember, it is the behavior that is bad—not the child. The child is still learning.

Know What to Expect

Ask the parents about their child's personality and what rules they want their child to abide by. Ask for suggestions on how to deal with any problems that might come up. Remember to read the Child's Personal Profile in chapter 7 of this manual for behavior patterns specific to the children in your care.

Super Sitters Tip •

Don't let favoritism affect your decisions with the children. Be fair.

Establish Control

You have a definite advantage. Although it may seem silly, the fact that you're taller and older makes you a very important person. You must make it clear from the beginning that you are in charge. But you don't have to do it in a threatening or scary way. *Never hit, spank, or slap a child.*

Set Clear, Realistic Limits

It's easier for a child when he or she knows what you expect. Ideally, your rules will be nearly the same as the parents' rules. Don't make any more rules than you need.

Be Consistent

It's confusing to a child if your rules keep changing. Always be fair. Children usually respond well to firm limits as long as the limits are consistent and fair.

Follow through Immediately

If you said you'd take the stick away if the child poked you again—do it. If you said you'd stop a game if the children didn't stop fighting, do it. It's important that the child knows you mean what you say.

Offer Choices

Children do not like being told what to do. You probably don't like being told what to do, either. Instead, offer the child positive choices that work within your rules: "If you don't want to share the blocks, you may do a puzzle or read a book." This way, you stay in control, and you give the child a chance to make a positive decision, and avoid a power struggle.

The Art of Distraction

One of the most effective ways to avoid or prevent problem behavior is to redirect the child's attention to something more positive and interesting.

Your job is to encourage behavior that helps children feel good about themselves. Never embarrass them.

About Babies

Babies are sensitive little people. Their digestive systems are delicate. Their muscles are still developing. Their bones are soft and so are the tops of their heads. Protect babies from bumps and falls. For young babies, you must always support their backs and heads. Babies get overheated and cold equally fast. Be aware of their body temperature and adjust. Don't over- or underdress them.

One to Two Months Old

Babies this age eat, sleep, burp, dirty their diapers, and need to be held a lot. Their food is mother's milk or formula and sometimes diluted fruit juice or water.

Colic is a problem for some babies. Colic is irritability and crying that's marked by sharp pains in the baby's intestine or immature digestive system. The baby may scream and cry, jerk his or her legs, and seem totally miserable. Often this fussiness occurs at the same time each day. Colicky babies need to be burped often during feedings. They need to be held, cuddled, and handled calmly. They often prefer to lie on their stomachs. Ask the parents for more helpful hints.

Three to Four Months Old

Now is the time babies frequently begin to smile. The baby is heavier, and most babies can now support their own heads. These babies enjoy lying on a blanket on their stomachs and looking at their surroundings and colorful toys. Feedings get easier. Babies this age know Mommy and Daddy from unfamiliar faces.

Four to Six Months Old

Because the baby now recognizes faces and voices, he or she knows the difference between Mom, Dad, and you. The baby may start to fuss for babysitters or respond more positively. At this age, they're more responsive to toys, colors, noises, and textures.

After Six Months

The baby can probably sit up and will be crawling before you know it. You'll probably enjoy the baby more, but you'll also have to be even more alert for his or her safety. Separation anxiety will probably be more intense, and babies experience pain from new teeth coming in.

Crying

Crying is normal for a baby. It's the baby's only way to communicate. You'll be able to recognize what the crying means as you get to know the baby better. Crying usually means the baby is:

- **Hungry.** Small babies cry desperately for food. Have the bottle ready in advance. Keep track of how long it's been since the last feeding.

- **Thirsty.** Especially during hot weather, the baby may need a drink of water or juice between feedings. Ask the parents what you should offer the baby to drink.

- **Sleepy.** Older babies get fussy but may be too busy to go to sleep. Gently rock the baby until he or she relaxes and falls off to sleep.

- **Gassy.** Young babies will cry when gas builds up after a feeding or before a bowel movement. Rub the baby's back to help him or her burp. The baby may spit up some food. *See pages 43–46 of this guide about feeding infants.*

- **Wet or dirty diaper.** Some babies hate to be wet, especially if they have a diaper rash. See page 42 of this guide for information on diapering.

- **Position.** Some babies have favorite ways to be held. Most like to lie on their stomachs. Some like to be cradled in your arm, or held up against your shoulder. Some babies like to sit up. Try supporting the baby on your lap, or putting him or her in an infant seat. Change positions until you find what works.

- **Teething.** When babies have new teeth growing through their gums, it hurts. Teething rings and chewable toys help. Do not give any medication unless instructed by the parents.

- **Boredom or overstimulation.** Vary activities. Include quiet play. Too much activity can become stressful. Calm the baby by rocking or singing. Walk the baby from room to room, and show him or her different shapes, colors, and sounds.

When nothing else seems to ease the baby's crying, check to see that there's nothing about the baby's clothing that's causing discomfort, like something binding too tightly or a little string caught between little toes.

Fussy times are not unusual for babies. Try to soothe the baby with cuddling, soft words, a quiet song, or perhaps a walk.

An older baby may miss his or her parents and be sad or upset for quite a while. Be compassionate, and keep the baby entertained.

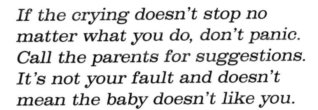

If the crying doesn't stop no matter what you do, don't panic. Call the parents for suggestions. It's not your fault and doesn't mean the baby doesn't like you.

Baby Safety

Never take your eyes off of a baby. It takes only a second for a baby to fall and get seriously hurt. Don't leave a baby alone on a changing table for even a second.

Babies put everything in their mouths. Keep your eyes open for small toys and objects, sharp toys, stones, buttons, pins, plastic bags, balloons. Keep these things away from the baby.

The hugs, kisses, and active play of an older child may be a little rough for a baby. Pushes and hits can hurt or frighten a baby, when an older child gets carried away. Be protective of the baby without being critical of the older child. Try to redirect the older child's attention to a more suitable and interesting activity. Sometimes roughness is an expression of the older child's jealousy and resentment over the attention a baby receives. The older child may be the one needing some special attention.

Never hold a baby with a hot drink in your hand. Don't hold the baby when you're working at the stove or carrying hot food.

Crawling babies find trouble. A Super Sitter finds the trouble first. Get down on the floor with the baby, and look for dangerous and tempting things like cords, electrical outlets, knickknacks, nut bowls and candy dishes, pet food bowls, tabletops with sharp corners, or lamps that might fall. *Never let a baby crawl out of sight.*

Diapers

Diapers are a fact of life until the baby is around two-and-a-half or three years old. Clean, dry diapers are important to the health and happiness of the child. Some children will cry when they're wet—some won't. So, you must check periodically.

Diaper rash is not uncommon and can be very painful. Change the child often, and be extra gentle while you clean him or her. Use ointment or petroleum jelly only as directed by the parents. Tell the parents about any rashes you see.

How to Diaper

If diapering is fairly new to you, then ask the parents to show you how they want the baby diapered, and practice in their presence.

Be sure the child is in a safe place, like the crib or playpen. Then gather everything you need, including extra clothes in case you make a mess. Remember: you can't leave the baby alone on the changing table. Be sure diaper pins are out of the baby's reach.

After you change a diaper, wash your hands before doing anything else.

Super Sitters Tip

• •

Before the parents leave, make sure they show you where to find everything for mealtime. Find out how to work appliances and highchairs. And locate favorite bibs, plates, cups, and spoons.

Mealtime with Infants

Bottles and bibs, spitting up, food on the floor, and messy faces: they're all part of feeding an infant. But actually, feeding an infant can be one of the most fun and rewarding parts of babysitting. Here's how to make mealtime enjoyable for both of you.

• If you've never fed an infant before, arrange a time to visit and observe how the parents do it.

• Relax. Infants are sensitive to the mood of the person caring for them. If you're confident and relaxed, it will help the infant to relax, and that will make for an easier, more enjoyable feeding.

• Refer to the Child's Personal Profile, menu, or other notes for instructions. Babies have tender tummies, so it's important to give the baby only foods approved by the parents. Foods are introduced to infants gradually and in special order to aid their digestion and test for allergies. So stick to what the parents tell you.

• Put the infant in a safe place. Then gather everything you need for the feeding: bottle, formula, nipple, and a towel for messy burps. When feeding the baby solid food, you will need baby food, dishes, baby spoon, and cloths or paper towels.

Bottle Feedings

Many infants drink formula for regular feedings. Never substitute milk for formula without the parents' approval. Water and juice may be offered between feedings, especially on hot days—but ask the parents first. Follow these steps for easy, relaxed bottle feedings:

- Ask the parents if they warm the formula. If yes, ask them how. Some parents use bottle warmers; others use warm water in a pan to heat the formula, and some use the bottle right out of the refrigerator or at room temperature.

- Always test the temperature of the formula before offering it to the infant. Formula that is too hot is dangerous. Gently shake the bottle to distribute the liquid evenly, and drip a few drops of formula onto the inside of your wrist. If it's comfortably warm on your wrist, it should be fine for the baby. If it's too hot, run some cool tap water over the bottle for a few seconds. Then test it again. If it's not warm enough, heat it a few seconds longer, and test it again.

- Select a comfortable chair, and hold the infant with his or her head resting comfortably on your supported arm. Be sure the baby's head is higher than the rest of his or her body.

  Relax. Talk softly to your little friend.

  Hold the bottle in your other hand with the bottom of the bottle higher than the nipple. Keep the neck of the bottle filled with formula to prevent air from getting into the infant's stomach. If the infant seems to have difficulty sucking, loosen the cover just a little bit. If he or she seems to be gulping too fast, tighten the cover slightly.

- Infants should be burped during and after every bottle feeding. They tend to get some air into their stomachs from sucking the nipple. There are two easy and effective ways to burp a baby:

1. Put a cloth diaper or towel on your shoulder. Gently lift the infant against your shoulder. Place the baby's face toward the diaper and be sure to support his or her head.

2. You can also sit the infant on your lap. Support the baby's head because most infants can't really sit yet. Have the extra cloth diaper or towel ready in your other hand.

Then, gently but firmly rub or pat the infant's back to help bring up the air bubbles. You'll hear one or two little burps. The infant may spit up some formula. Don't worry; a little spitup is normal.

Infants are all different. Some need to be burped after every two ounces of formula they drink. Others only need to burp about halfway through their bottle and again when they're finished. Ask the parents what they recommend. Interrupting the feeding too often is frustrating and unpleasant to the baby.

How much should an infant drink at each bottle feeding? Ask the parents. Most babies stop feeding when they're full.

Baby Food

Ask the parents if the infant usually gets the food first or the bottle first, and stay with the usual routine. Put everything you need near the high chair, and brace yourself for a mess.

- Remember the bib and wash cloth! You'll need them.

- Put the infant in the infant seat or high chair. *Use the safety belt.*

- Offer the infant only foods approved by the parents.

Infants sometimes push the food out of their mouths almost as often as you put it in. Be patient and keep trying. And give the baby only as much as the parents indicate. Don't worry if the infant doesn't finish his or her portion.

Playing with Babies

Babies sometimes get bored. After a few minutes, they get tired, fussy, or disinterested. Here are some favorite baby games:

- Imitate baby sounds, and you may get smiles and gurgles in return.

- Babies enjoy things that move. They love to watch colorful mobiles.

- Make funny, silly faces—not scary. Use lots of smiles. They love to reach up and touch your nose, eyes, and mouth.

- Shine a flashlight on a wall and move it around slowly. Make sure the room is only a little dark.

- Babies like fingers and toes—theirs and yours. They'll grab your fingers and put them in their mouths—so keep yours clean.

- Sing nursery rhymes. Play records or tapes of soothing music. Dance gently to the music.

- Some babies like to be tickled—very gently like a feather. Baby's first reaction will tell you if he or she likes it. If the baby doesn't like it, stop.

- Take a tour of the house. Show the baby brightly colored objects, things that move, views out the window, pictures and photographs, and ticking clocks. Tell the baby the names of the objects.

- Peek-a-boo is still a hit with babies six months old or older.

- Lay the baby on a blanket on the floor and put some simple, safe toys within reach.

One-Year-Olds

Almost everything is fun for these little ones. Crawl with them. Lay them on your chest. They love to roll over. Help them walk if they're ready. Stack blocks and have the child knock them down. One-year-olds love to drop things and see how they fall. Your part of this game is to pick the things up and give them back to the child. You'll get tired of this game long before the child will!

If there's a playpen in the house, ask the parents when the baby likes to play in it and how long he or she usually is content there. Check the playpen to make sure no small, sharp, or dangerous objects have accidently found their way inside.

How to Bathe a Baby

Bathe infants very carefully. They are slippery and totally helpless. Do not give a baby a bath unless you're sure you know what to do and the parents insist that you do it. Ask the parents to let you come and see how they bathe the baby. Find out what time the baby usually gets his or her bath. Locate the tub, a bathinette, a sink, or a plastic tub.

Your confidence will help the baby relax and enjoy the bath. Just follow these easy steps:

- Put the baby in a safe place like the crib or playpen and gather everything you need: towels, washcloth, bath mat, soap, shampoo, toys, and clothes or pajamas.

- Put all dangerous and potentially poisonous objects in the bathroom out of the child's reach, especially electrical appliances.

- Just a few inches of water in the tub or bathinette is enough.

- Use your elbow to be sure the water is just lukewarm—babies can be badly burned by water that is too hot. Test the water *before* you put the baby in.

- Smile and talk to the baby while you undress him or her. Support the baby's head and shoulders if he or she can't yet sit. Gradually put the baby in the water. Never let go—always keep one hand on the baby, even if the child sits well. Continue to talk and smile.

- Never leave a child alone in the bath. Let the telephone ring. Ignore the doorbell. A few seconds and a few inches of water are enough for disaster.

- Keeping one hand on the baby, use your free hand to gently soap him or her. Use very little soap. Don't put soap or much water on the baby's head or face—simply wipe them gently with a warm, wrung out washcloth.

- Rinse the soap off thoroughly to prevent chafing and rashes—especially under the folds of baby fat.

- Carefully lift the baby out of the water. Wrap the baby in a towel so he or she won't get cold. Dry the baby, and apply powder or lotion as directed by the parents. Diaper and dress the baby.

> *Avoid using powder unless the parents insist. If you must use powder, avoid creating a cloud of powder because it's not good for the baby to breathe it in.*

A sponge bath is a good substitute for a tub bath. It's also good when the child has a fever or an especially messy bowel movement. Gather everything you need near the changing table or waterproof pad. Undress the baby and wrap him or her in a towel. Wash and dry one part of the baby's body at a time with warm water and wash cloth. Dry quickly to prevent the child from becoming chilled. Clean up the bath area while the baby naps.

Bedtime and Babies

Most babies fall asleep when they're tired. Don't give them a pillow; they could smother themselves. Some babies fuss a while before nodding off. If the baby has trouble falling asleep, try one of these suggestions.

- Gently rub the baby's back.

- Play or sing soothing music.

- Rock the baby.

- Walk the baby until he or she falls asleep.

Ask parents about favorite sleeping positions, special blankets, toys, pacifiers, mobiles, and music boxes. Find out when the baby normally sleeps—and for how long. Check the Child's Profile. If the baby wakes up suddenly and needs help going back to sleep, find out what you should do.

Tell the parents about any bedtime problems.

About Toddlers

Toddlers have lots of energy and curiosity and often get into mischief. They love to explore. Since they haven't yet learned their limitations, it's up to you to be nearby watching and helping them discover the world.

Separation Anxiety

Many toddlers will start to cry the minute you walk in. They'll probably calm down, and then they'll start up again when Mom and Dad head for the door. It's not that they don't like you; it's just that your arriving means Mommy and Daddy are leaving. Don't take the tears personally. It will pass. You can help by gently reassuring the child and distracting him or her with interesting activities. Sometimes, there is little you can do except continue your reassurance.

"Help Me" versus "Leave Me Alone"

Toddlers sometimes don't know what they want. One minute they want your help, the next minute they're screaming because they want to do something themselves. Stay nearby and be ready to step in, but be patient. Give toddlers plenty of time to put on their socks, do a puzzle, put away their toys, or whatever. Praise their efforts, don't get frustrated, and try not to let the children get too frustrated either.

Temper Tantrums

Toddlers may kick and scream for no obvious reason. Be calm. You can't reason with most children at this age. The tantrum will pass. Just be sure the children can't hurt themselves. Show mild concern and attention until the child settles down. When all is calm, continue with your care of the child.

Toddlers Don't Know How to Share

One of the toddler's favorite words is "mine". Be alert for pushing and other aggressive behavior between brothers and sisters or playmates. Even hugs can turn into tears when they get rough.

Setting Limits

As a sitter, it is sometimes difficult to define "unacceptable behavior" because you don't know the family's rules. Super Sitters defines "unacceptable behavior" as things that are unsafe or harmful to the child or those around the child.

Toddlers need to know that you will not allow unacceptable behavior. They may not understand the reason, but you must teach them through firm, gentle, and consistent actions that you mean business. When you want a child to stop doing something, distract him or her with an interesting new toy or activity.

Scolding may not work. Repeat your rules as often as necessary, and remove the child from danger as many times as it takes. Interest the child in a safer activity. Be firm. Be consistent. Ask the parents what they do when their child misbehaves so you can be consistent with their rules. Never spank or hit a child, even if the child's parents permit it.

Toddler Safety

Never let a toddler out of your sight. Stay close, and be ready to move quickly. Keep your eyes open for potential danger. Toddlers are just beginning to know their limitations—and you may not know their capabilities. Hold hands to cross streets, and carry the child across if he or she tends to pull away from you.

Toilet Training

Most children learn to use the toilet sometime after their second birthday. Be helpful. Be positive. Praise and encourage. Never scold or embarrass the child. Remember that the child is just learning.

Parents should tell you exactly how they are teaching the child to use the toilet, and how to tell when the child needs to go to the bathroom. Watch for signs like crossed legs, hands between the legs, or a sudden stop in play.

Mistakes can happen—sometimes the child doesn't make it to the toilet or simply forgets to go. Help the child change clothes and suggest to the child that he or she use the potty next time. Toddlers are very sensitive. Never make them feel that any part of their bodies is dirty or bad.

Report toilet training accidents to the parents when the child is not listening.

Mealtime with Toddlers

Toddlers Are Independent

Your job is to be watchful and keep the child safe from falling and choking. Children are likely to climb into their booster chairs, grab a cup, and start eating with their fingers. Give children only foods approved by the parents. Expect messes, and keep mealtime fun.

Weaning from the Bottle

Even a child who drinks from a cup may want a bottle for comfort when Mommy and Daddy are away. Unless the parents object, let the child have it.

Playing with Toddlers

While you're playing, keep your eyes open for breakable and dangerous things. Here are some favorite toddler activities:

- Toddlers love to chase sitters. They'll run after you with squeals of delight. Let them catch you after a little chase. If you chase them, keep it fun and nonthreatening.

- Hide-and-seek is a favorite game. Let the children see the direction in which you are going to hide. Then tell them to find you, and watch their animated faces as they discover you.

- "Fill, empty, and pour" keeps toddlers happy and has endless possibilities. Use things that toddlers won't choke on. Pouring water is great fun—if parents don't mind.

- Sit on the floor together, spread your legs, and roll a ball.

- Make musical instruments from boxes, pots and pans, paper towel rolls, wooden spoons. Have a parade. Play along with records.

- Toddlers enjoy make-believe trips to the store, the zoo, and grandma's house. Pretend to cook and serve a meal.

Super Sitters Tip •

When you're outside, be alert for strangers. If you suspect trouble, don't be afraid to call for help.

- Almost all toddlers love books. Read stories. Make up stories. Books of nursery rhymes, fairy tales that aren't scary, and picture books are good, quiet fun. They also help the young children learn about the world and learn the words to describe what they see.

- Building blocks are great.

- Help the child learn the ABC's, colors, and shapes. Pay more attention to the answers the child gets right than to the mistakes.

- You may want to bring along a little toy that comes and goes with you. The child will enjoy it—and will have something to look forward to each time you visit.

- Play outside. You can go for walks and stroller rides, run around, discover swings and sand boxes. Exploring trees, flowers, and insects can keep a toddler happily occupied for a while. Stay close and be ready to prevent accidents, especially around climbing toys, slides, steps, and on uneven ground. If a child falls, be ready to catch him or her. Hold hands or carry the child across streets.

Take emergency telephone numbers with you—and coins for a pay phone.

If the toddler is learning to use the toilet, try to stay near one. Have the child use the toilet before going outside. You may want to take extra clothes with you to the park.

How to Bathe a Toddler

Be sure to gather everything you need before you put the child in the tub: washcloth, bath mat, soap, shampoo, towel, and clothes or pajamas. Never put more than a few inches of water in the tub. Always check the water temperature before the child goes in the tub. Lift the child into the tub, or hold on to him or her to prevent slips. Be alert, and don't leave the toddler alone for a second.

Most toddlers love bath time. Be sure to put *safe* toys in the tub (never anything made of glass), and allow time for play.

Washing hair isn't easy. Skip it unless the parents insist. If you must wash the child's hair, try using a wet washcloth. Be sure to put your hand above the child's eyes to catch the drips. Or, put an inch of water in the tub, and have the child lie carefully on his or her back. While you support the child's head with one hand, gently wash the child's hair with the other. Rinse completely. Dry hair thoroughly with a towel.

Lift the child out of the tub—don't let the child climb.

Bedtime for Toddlers

Toddlers usually have regular bedtimes, but they don't always want to go to bed. Use your Super Sitters playtime skills to find quiet games and activities just before bedtime. Check the Child's Profile for bedtime snacks and routines, special blankets or stuffed animals, night lights, and favorite stories or songs.

Some toddlers have trouble falling asleep. You may have to read them several stories or, if the parents allow it, you may let them doze off in front of the TV. Sometimes a child may refuse to sleep until the parents come home. The first time you sit, you may have to allow it until you have a chance to talk with the parents. Discuss the situation with them when they return and suggest that they tell the child what he or she must do at bedtime. Be patient. Let the parents know about any bedtime problems, especially if they happen every time you sit. Parents may have some other helpful hints.

About Older Children

Three- to Four-Year-Olds

Children at this age are beginning to learn right from wrong. They're very sensitive about making mistakes, so try not to scold, embarrass them, or make them feel guilty. Keep your temper even when the children lose theirs. Try to be forgiving.

By the time they're three years old, many children are capable of sharing and cooperative play.

Four- to Five-Year-Olds

When children have reached this age, they are generally more mature, good listeners, curious, and somewhat independent. They are usually more complex than three- to four-year-olds, and you can begin to reason with them.

Allow them a chance to be independent. Give them plenty of time to dress themselves or do their own art project. Give choices, and let them help make decisions. You might, for example, let the child choose between riding a bike or going to the park—or between soup and a sandwich or yogurt and applesauce for lunch. Try to be patient, and discover how much independence this child can handle.

Five- to Seven-Year-Olds

Children at this age generally need and want less attention from a sitter. They often prefer to play alone or with a friend, so give them the chance, and stay reasonably close.

Older children may resist your authority. Be firm but understanding.

Safety for Older Children

Older children have already learned a lot about danger, but curiosity will continue to lead them into things they know nothing about. Watch for new dangers—like a sharp knife, scissors, or playground equipment that the child hasn't quite mastered. Scan play areas for potential danger, and stay close enough to step in for safety's sake.

Mealtime with Older Children

Older children often enjoy setting the table and preparing the food. Help make it fun, but keep it safe. Let them help clean up, too. Be sure to check the Child's Profile for food allergies and favorite things to eat.

Playing with Older Children

A Super Sitter makes playtime fun, educational, and relaxing for the children. The main thing is to get involved in those activities that the child enjoys. Playtime is a great time to help older children learn about words, numbers, nature, and safety. Helping the child with homework can be fun and rewarding for both of you.

Energy and imagination give older children plenty of their own ideas for playtime.

Before the parents leave, ask them if playmates are allowed in the house or yard while they're away.

Rainy, indoor days can be difficult, so be ready with some of your own new ideas. Here are a few suggestions that are easily adaptable as the child grows older:

- Make-believe games intrigue most older children. Props and costumes add to the activity. Don't hesitate to create adventures.

- Puzzles, books, games, coloring, cut and paste, and modeling clay are good quiet activities.

- Make a book. Help the child make up a story. Write it down for the child, and allow him or her to draw the pictures. Cut out pictures from old magazines— you might want to bring some along.

Super Sitters Tip •

Take a house key along when you go outside. Put a few bandages in your pocket, and emergency phone numbers, including where the parents can be reached. Use sunscreen and insect repellent as directed by the parents. Avoid overheating. Offer lots of drinks in hot weather.

• Give the child freedom to run and explore. Stay within sight, and be ready to run. Play catch, baseball, kickball, or tag. Explore nature. Go to the park. Make nature pictures with sticks, stones, leaves, and sand.

Super Sitter's Fun Bag

Super Sitters plan ahead. Nothing is more entertaining for children than things that are new and different. Bring your own bag of things when you babysit. Fill it with things you enjoy, things that are just right for the ages of the children. Here are some suggestions:

Old magazines	Blunt scissors
Glue/glue stick	Old socks
Paper lunch bags	Colored yarn
Washable markers	Cotton balls
Construction paper	Bits of cloth
Tennis balls	Table-tennis balls
Puppets	Records/tapes
Books	Poems
Magnifying glass	

If you need new ideas for things to do, your library has many activity books for children of all ages.

Older Children and Bath Time

Stay nearby. If the child demands privacy, stay outside the bathroom door and listen for trouble. Test the water temperature before the child gets in—and be available if the child needs a hand getting in or out of the tub. Allow for playtime.

Safety is the most important thing about bath time with children of all ages. Be sure to take all necessary precautions. Because of the dangers involved and because of concern for the child's privacy, we suggest parents bathe their children and not give sitters this responsibility. If the parents insist, make sure they leave specific instructions.

Bedtime and Older Children

Check the Child's Profile for bedtime routines and rules. Some children know when they're tired and will go to bed willingly. Others will resist even though they're tired, and with these children you must be firm but gentle. Negotiating for five more minutes of playtime or another story is normal, but when you make a deal, stick with it.

Always avoid scary fairy tales and bedtime stories. Many children have a fear of the dark, imagine monsters under beds and in closets, and have nightmares. A child cannot always tell the difference between fantasy and reality. If a child does become frightened, respond to the fears with the reassurance that you will protect the child. Check the Child's Profile for any special bedtime routines. We recommend that you try a little drink of water, tuck the child in, say goodnight, and stay with the child until he or she falls off to sleep. Of course, you should follow whatever routine the parents advise.

Keeping Cool in Emergencies

Things go wrong. The child in your care is counting on you to know what to do. Because you're a Super Sitter, you're prepared for just about anything. The most important thing to do in any emergency is to stay calm.

When you're calm, you can think clearly. Read through the Super Sitters First Aid and Emergency Care Manual. The introduction offers good instruction on how to act in an emergency.

> *If you're prepared, it's easier to stay calm. And when you're calm, the child feels safer.*

Going Home

Make sure the house is at least as tidy as you found it. Give the parents a complete report on how things were during your sitting time. Tell them about anything unusual that happened or any problems. And give them the telephone messages.

After you've been paid, it's time to go home. Be sure you get home safely. Don't let a drunk parent drive you home. If you're concerned for any reason about being driven home, call your parents to pick you up. They won't mind.

Using the Super Sitters Forms

You now know how important you are to the happiness and well-being of the children in your care. The Super Sitters forms that follow are specially designed to provide you with the information you need to be an outstanding sitter.

Read through the forms now. Learn all you can about the children. Think about how you'll react in different situations with them. With the help of these forms, you'll be prepared to do a great job.

And remember to refer to the forms whenever you have a question or when an emergency arises.

7

Child's Personal Profile

Why Use These Forms?

Each child is unique with special needs and habits. Each child has favorite foods, special things he or she takes to bed to make bedtime feel safe, special words that are comforting when the child is afraid.

Children are happiest when life follows all the little routines they know. Because you care for the child every once in a while, you may not be familiar with these routines. You may not know about the favorite cup or plate that *must* be used at mealtime. Or bedtime can be endless hours of crying because you didn't know about a special blanket or favorite story that's *always* read.

The Child's Personal Profile contains the important details you need to put the child at ease and to make your babysitting time with the child safe and fun.

> *Take a few minutes to look it over. It'll always be there when you need it.*

Bedtime and Nap Time

Must the child take a nap? _____

_____

What time is nap time for each child? _____

_____

How long is nap time? _____

_____

What should I do if the child won't sleep? (Can he or
she just lie quietly? May the child read a book or play
in his or her room? Should I lie down with the child?)

_____

Does the child sleep on his or her back or stomach? ____

_____

Does the child use a pacifier? _____

Where is it? _____

Does the child have a special doll, toy, or blanket for
nap time/bedtime? _____

_____

Should the door be open or shut? _____

_____

Does the child nap with the lights on or off? _____

What is bedtime for each child? _____

_____

Bedtime and Nap Time continued

Where are the child's pajamas? _____

Is there a bedtime snack? _____

Is the child afraid of the dark? _____

Monsters? _____ Thunder? _____

How are fears consoled? _____

_____

Do I need to awaken the child to take him or her to
the toilet? _____

How often? _____ When? _____

Are there any prayers or blessings that should be said
at bedtime? _____

_____

Are there any other bedtime routines? _____

_____

_____

_____

_____

_____

_____

_____

_____

_____

Mealtime

Are there any food allergies? _____

If yes, what reactions should I watch for, and what
should I do if a reaction occurs? _____

_____

_____

Are there any overall dietary concerns? (Vegetarian,
Kosher, No salt, No sugar, Other?) _____

_____

_____

When is mealtime? Breakfast: _____

Lunch: _____   Dinner: _____

Are there special dishes, spoons, or bibs? _____

_____

Does the child feed himself/herself? _____

What should the child eat? _____

_____

_____

Is there anything the child should *not* eat? _____

_____

_____

May the child watch TV while eating? _____

_____

Mealtime continued

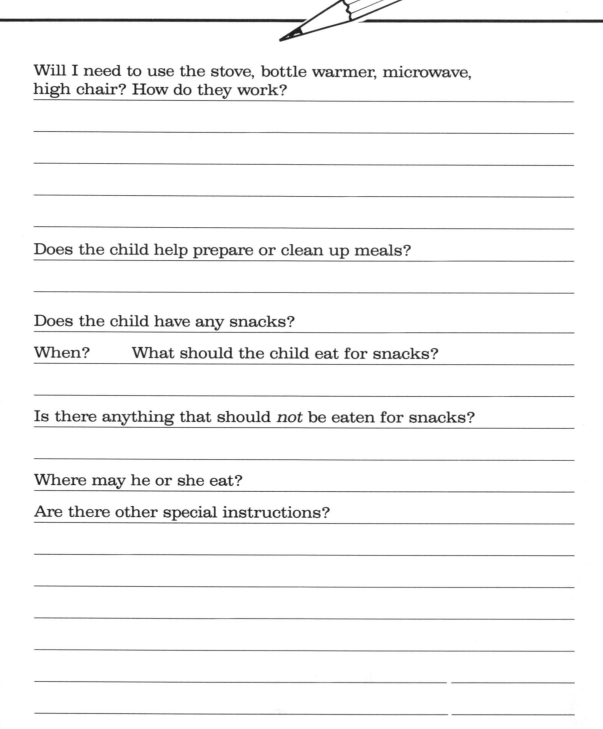

Will I need to use the stove, bottle warmer, microwave, high chair? How do they work?

_____

_____

_____

_____

Does the child help prepare or clean up meals?

_____

Does the child have any snacks?

_____

When?   What should the child eat for snacks?

_____

Is there anything that should *not* be eaten for snacks?

_____

Where may he or she eat?

_____

Are there other special instructions?

_____

_____

_____

_____

_____

_____

Bottle Feeding and Infant Foods

What does the baby take in his or her bottle? Milk?
Formula?
_____

Should the bottle be heated, room temperature, or
straight from the refrigerator?
_____

If heated, how do you heat the bottle?
_____

_____

_____

How often does the baby take a bottle or eat? (Any
regular schedule? Anytime the baby seems hungry?
_____

_____

Does the baby eat any solid foods yet?
_____

_____

Are there other special instructions for feeding
your baby?
_____

_____

_____

_____

_____

_____

_____

_____

_____

Indoor Play

In what rooms does the child play?

_____

Are any rooms "off limits"?

_____

What are the child's favorite toys, games, activities?

_____

_____

_____

Where are the smocks or old clothes for messy
projects like painting and pasting?

_____

May we cook or bake?

_____

May we watch TV? (VCR)   When?

_____

Where?

_____

What programs (tapes) may the child watch?

_____

Are any programs forbidden?

_____

May the child turn on the TV without help?

_____

How are arguments over toys usually handled?

_____

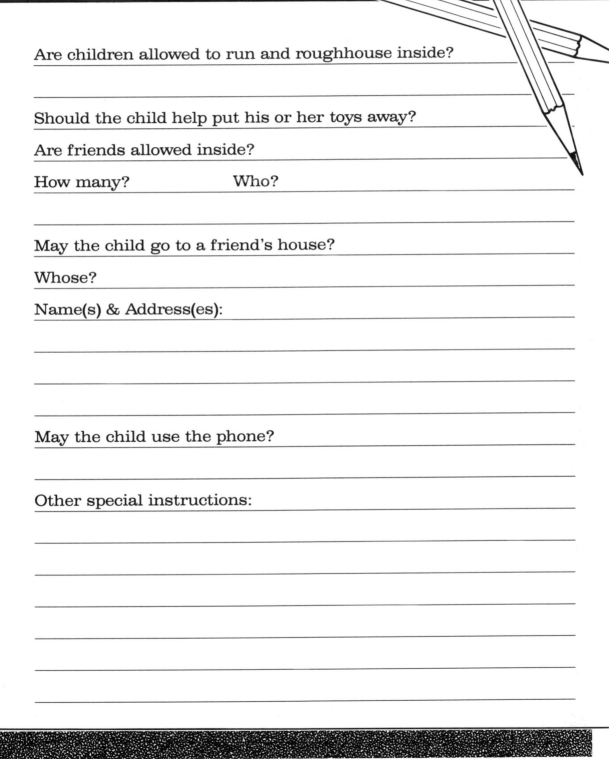

Are children allowed to run and roughhouse inside? _____

_____

Should the child help put his or her toys away? _____

Are friends allowed inside? _____

How many? _____ Who? _____

_____

May the child go to a friend's house? _____

Whose? _____

Name(s) & Address(es): _____

_____

_____

_____

May the child use the phone? _____

_____

Other special instructions: _____

_____

_____

_____

_____

_____

_____

Outdoor Play

Where does the child play: front yard, back yard, park?

_____

Are any areas off limits?

_____

What are the child's favorite toys, games, activities?

_____

Are there any special rules for outside?

_____

Are friends allowed outside?

How many? _____ Who? _____

May the child go to a friend's house?

Who?

Name(s), address(es), phone:

_____

Are insect bites a problem?

(How should bites be treated?)

_____

Other outdoor play concerns:

_____

Bath Time and Toilet

Is a bath needed?   When? _____

Do children bathe together? _____

Where are the child's towels? _____

Soap?   Shampoo? _____

Is the child fearful in the tub? _____

Do I stay in the bathroom with the older children? _____

What toys are allowed in the tub? _____

_____

How long does bath time usually last? _____

Does the child know how to lock the door? _____

How can the bathroom door be unlocked from
the outside? _____

_____

Is the child toilet trained? _____

In the process of learning? _____

Where are diapers?   Training pants? _____

_____

Should I use lotion or powder? _____

Other special toileting or diapering concerns: _____

_____

Other Special Needs of My Child:

Location of Emergency and First Aid Items

fire extinguisher: _____

flashlight: _____

candles & matches: _____

bandages & antiseptic: _____

cotton/gauze/tape: _____

syrup of ipecac (for poisoning): _____

pain & fever reliever: _____

cough medication: _____

medicine spoon: _____

insect bite lotion: _____

sunscreen: _____

thermometer: _____

other: _____

_____

_____

_____

_____

DO NOT GIVE MEDICATION UNLESS INSTRUCTED BY PARENTS OR DOCTOR

Location of Household Items

matches: _____

thermostat & instructions: _____

extra keys: _____

bathroom key: _____

cleaning supplies: _____

vacuum/broom/mop: _____

trash bags: _____

circuit breakers/fuse/fuse box: _____

gas shut off: _____

gas company phone number: _____

water shut off: _____

plumber: _____

petty cash: _____

door alarms & security system: _____

other: _____

_____

_____

_____

_____

_____

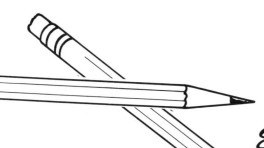

Emergency Phone Numbers

You are at: _____

family name: _____

address: _____

telephone: _____

fire: _____ police: _____

doctor: _____

home #: _____ office #: _____

rescue squad: _____

poison: _____

taxi: _____

child's name: _____

age: _____

child's name: _____

age: _____

Mother's work: _____

Father's work: _____

preferred hospital: _____

address: _____

telephone: _____

_____

_____

First Aid and Emergency Care

Bedside Manner

Bedside manner is the right balance of first aid and medical skill with tender loving care. It's knowing what to do and remaining calm enough to do it. In addition to proper medical attention, there's nothing more effective than genuine caring and sympathy to make a child feel better.

In life-threatening or other emergency situations, quick calm action is the first priority. Use this first aid manual, and do what you can. Get help immediately. Every second counts.

With minor injuries, you need to attend to everything: the hurt knee, the hurt feelings, and the fear. Let the child know you understand that he or she hurts and is unhappy. Some people get so caught up attending to the injury that they forget about the child. A Super Sitter remembers to care for both. Your calm concern will help the child get through the few minutes of discomfort with the minimum of tears, fear, and anguish.

When the child isn't feeling well, many of the same techniques you find successful at bedtime and playtime will help. A favorite story, some soothing songs, that special teddy bear, or a favorite activity can do wonders. And most important, your patience, compassion, sympathy, and good humor are essential. You know what it's like to be sick. Try to remember how you felt when you were young and what was comforting to you.

Keeping Calm

In an emergency, you're in charge. Every minute counts. Your cool-headed thinking and fast action could save a child's life.

It's natural for you to be a little frightened in an emergency. Take a deep breath, and think about what must be done. Quickly find the page in this manual that will tell you exactly what to do. Get help if help is required. Act quickly.

Remember that the child may be more frightened than you are. While you're dealing with the emergency, try to be reassuring with the child. Help him or her feel that you're in control and that you know just what to do. When you're calm, it will help the child to be calm, and a calm child is much easier for you to handle.

Getting Help

This handbook will tell you whom to call first: parents, doctor, or rescue squad. Ask the parents where you can find these numbers quickly.

> *When the child's life or limb is at stake, get help immediately.*

Call the rescue squad. If you're outside at a park or other public place, get help from a nearby adult, neighbor, or bystander. DON'T LEAVE THE CHILD if at all possible. Send an adult or older child to call for help.

When to Call the Parents

If the illness or injury seems at all serious, if you're worried, or if you're just not quite sure what to do—call the parents. Parents would rather you called them, even if they decide the situation is not so serious. Let *them* decide if they need to come home.

It's better to be overcautious. When in doubt, call. If you can't reach the parents and you're worried, call the doctor.

When to Call the Doctor

There are times when you should call the doctor even before you call the parents. Use this list of emergencies to help you decide when to call the doctor. Call the doctor for the following injuries.

- Serious cuts with lots of blood, large wounds, or wounds that won't stop bleeding

- Burns

- Something in the eye, ear, or nose

- Something sharp that has been swallowed

- Severe or prolonged pain

- Possible broken bones

When to Call the Rescue Squad

Call the rescue squad immediately if the child is in the following state:

- Unconscious

- Having difficulty breathing or not breathing at all

- Bleeding severely and you cannot stop the blood, or if the child has lost a lot of blood

- Choking

- Has a severely broken bone

When in doubt, call.

Poison Control

If you suspect poison has been swallowed, call poison control.

Talking on the Phone in an Emergency

Have a paper and pencil handy to write down any instructions you are given. Give this information clearly:

1 Give the address or location you're at and the phone number you're calling from. EXAMPLE:
I need help at _____ (address or location).
The phone number is _____.

2 Describe the emergency. EXAMPLE:
A _____-year old child fell, and I think the child broke his (her) leg.

3 Identify yourself, and give the name of the family. EXAMPLE:
I'm Jenny Brown, the babysitter. I'm at the (name of child's family) home.

Wait for any instructions before hanging up. Write them down and repeat them to be sure you understand what to do. Do not hang up until the person on the other end of the line hangs up first. That way you'll be sure not to miss any important questions or information.

Super Sitters Tip

• •

Make sure you know the name, address, and phone number of the house where you are sitting. You don't want to have to run outside to look for the address when making an emergency call.

First Aid and Medical Care

Medication

> *Never give any medication unless you've been told to do so by the parents, doctor, or poison control center.*

1 Have the parents leave you exact written instructions.

2 If you are receiving instructions over the phone, write down the exact name of the medication, the correct dosage, and how often the medication should be given to the child.

3 Read the instructions back to the parents, doctor, or poison control center to make sure you have it right.

4 Measure the dosage exactly. Use a medicine spoon or measuring spoon.

5 Close the cap on the medication securely, and put it out of the child's reach.

Getting the Child to Take the Medicine

Ask the parents for helpful ways to ensure that the child takes the whole dosage.

Here Are Some Ideas:

1 For infants, use a clean dropper. Do not mix medication into formula, juice, or water since the infant may not get the full dose.

2 Most older children will cooperate. If you have problems, ask the parents if it's okay to crush the pills and bury them in applesauce or jam.

> *If you're not sure about the medication or the dosage, call the parents or the doctor.*

Allergic Reactions

> *Minor reaction (itching, rash): Call the parents. Difficulty breathing or severe vomiting: Call the rescue squad.*

Parents should tell you about any serious allergies affecting the child. See Child's Personal Profile. Be sure to ask about appropriate treatment should an allergic reaction occur.

Unexpected Allergic Reactions

Symptoms

1 Runny nose and eyes, sneezes, cough

2 Breathing difficulty, wheezing

3 Skin rash, hives

4 Vomiting

What to do

1 If the reaction is minor, call the parents immediately for instructions.

2 To relieve itching, bathe the child in warm water mixed with one cup of baking soda. Ask the parents first.

3 For severe breathing difficulties or vomiting, call the rescue squad immediately.

Do not give any medication unless instructed to do so by the doctor or the parents.

Sickness (Colds, Flu)

Call the parents if sickness begins while you are sitting or if the child's condition worsens.

There is not much that can be done except to make the child as comfortable as possible.

1 Do not give any medication unless specifically instructed to do so by the parents or the doctor.

2 Keep the child indoors. Be sure the child is comfortably warm but not too hot.

3 Give the child plenty of fluids to drink (only those recommended by the parents). If the child has the flu, ask the parents for specific food instructions.

4 Play quietly. Read stories. Listen to records. Be sure the child rests. Remember, when a child is sick, he or she needs your extra special care and attention. Think back to a time when you were sick and what made you comfortable, and you'll know just what to do.

Fever or Vomiting

> *Call parents if a fever comes on quickly or gets higher, or if the child vomits frequently.*

1 For vomiting, clean the child and make him or her comfortable. Use a lukewarm, damp cloth to wipe face and hands.

2 Do not give any medication unless instructed to do so.

3 **Call the parents if symptoms begin after the parents have left or if they get worse. If you cannot reach the parents, call the doctor.**

4 Do not take the child's temperature unless you've been requested by the parents to do so and have been told how to do it properly and safely.

5 Refer to Fever, page 87, and Vomiting, page 93.

6 Fever and vomiting require special skill and concern. Pay attention to the child's feelings. Calm and assure the child. And never shame a child for throwing up. He or she is already feeling rotten enough physically; try to keep the child feeling okay in every other way.

Cuts and Scrapes

> *Stop the bleeding, clean and bandage the wound, and comfort the child.*

1 Use a clean bandage, cloth, or towel to apply gentle but firm pressure to the wound until bleeding stops (two to five minutes). Add another cloth on top of the first if necessary—don't release the pressure.

2 When the bleeding stops, gently wash the wound with soap and water. Apply antiseptic to the bandage, and bandage firmly. (It is less painful to the child if you apply antiseptic to the bandage instead of directly to the wound.)

3 If there is glass or another sharp object in the wound, or if the wound looks very deep or wide, call the parents.

Comfort the child as you care for the injury. Watch for any new bleeding.

Be sure to tell the parents what happened and what steps you took.

Earache

> *Call the parents. If you can't reach the parents, call the doctor.*

Earaches and ear infections can be quite painful. A child may poke, pull, or rub the ear if it aches, and cry in shrieks of pain.

Unexpected Earache

1 Call the parents. If you can't reach the parents, call the doctor.

2 Do not give any medication unless specifically instructed to do so by the parents or the doctor. Follow instructions carefully.

3 Earaches are extremely painful to children. They may cry uncontrollably. If they awaken in the night, they may be very tired yet unable to sleep because of the pain. When they are little, there is often little to do except hold and rock them. If you have been given permission to give them a pain reliever, it will generally work in about twenty minutes. Normally the child will then fall asleep until the medication wears off (in about four hours). You will need to be patient with the child until the medication takes effect or until the parents come home. Be kind, gentle, and reassuring. If you start to get frustrated or impatient with the child's crying, maybe you can find a song to sing that will help soothe you both. A Super Sitter always places the child first, no matter how difficult or frustrating the situation.

Ear Injury

1 If there is any possibility of injury to the inner ear, or if you notice any drainage from the ear, call the parents or the doctor immediately.

2 Treat the outer ear only. Stop the bleeding, and clean and protect the wound.

Object in Ear

1 **Do not try to remove the object with your fingers.**

2 Tip the child's head to the side. If the object does not fall out, call the parents or the doctor. You may need to take the child to the doctor or hospital.

Fever

> *Call the parents if fever begins unexpectedly or becomes higher. Call the parents or doctor anytime an infant develops a fever.*

The child will feel noticeably warm to the touch and will appear ill.

You should not take the child's temperature unless specifically instructed to do so. Never take a child's temperature rectally unless you have been taught the correct procedure; you could injure the child.

What to Do

1 Do not give the child any medication unless you have been told to do so.

2 Call the parents if the fever comes on unexpectedly or becomes high. A normal oral temperature is 98.6. For temperatures of over 100°, call the parents or the doctor.

3 If instructed by the parents, you can give the child plenty of cool liquids to drink.

4 Gently wipe the child's face, neck, and arms with a *lukewarm* cloth. If the fever is very high, the parents or doctor may ask you to bathe the child in *lukewarm* water. Never use cold water—it causes chills. Follow all bath time instructions on pages 47–49.

5 Be sure the child is not dressed too warmly. Avoid drafts and chills.

6 If the fever seems very high, and you cannot reach the parents, call the doctor.

7 Have the child rest or play quietly. Try reading stories and playing records or tapes.

8 A child with a fever feels sick. His or her resistance is down, physically and emotionally. He or she may be more sensitive than usual. BE KIND AND GENTLE.

Diarrhea

> *Call the parents if diarrhea is severe.*
> *Call the doctor if the parents cannot be reached.*

Breast-fed infants and other infants not yet getting solid foods often have loose bowel movements. This is normal, not diarrhea.

What to Do

1 Clean up the child gently, calming the child as you go along. Get clean clothes as needed. No one likes the mess, but stay calm. Try not to further upset the child by letting him or her know how much you dislike cleaning up the mess.

2 With infants and babies you may need to use ointment to prevent diaper rash. Ask the parents. If the parents have not instructed you on the proper use of the ointment, call them and ask.

3 Do not give the child milk or other dairy products, fruits, or fruit juice. Offer the child small amounts of water.

4 Do not give any medication unless told to do so.

5 Call the parents. Tell them how many times the child has had diarrhea, if there was blood or pus in it, and if the child has a fever or any other symptoms. Ask for special instructions regarding food and drinks.

If diarrhea seems severe and you cannot reach the parents, call the doctor.

Nosebleeds

If the bleeding won't stop, call the parents.
If you cannot reach the parents quickly, call the doctor.

Remember that the child is scared. Your calm concern is important here.

Do not let the child lie down—the child may choke on the blood.
Keep the child sitting up.

What to Do

1 Help the child to sit erect.

2 Firmly but gently pinch the outside of the nose just below the eyes until the bleeding stops (5 minutes).

3 Talk calmly to the child to help him or her relax. When the bleeding stops, gently clean the child's face, and get clean clothes if needed. Have the child play quietly to avoid additional bleeding. Play a quiet game. Read stories. Listen to records. Color.

4 Be sure to tell the parents what happened.

Something in the Ear or Nose

> *If you can't see the object, leave it alone and call the parents. If you cannot reach the parents quickly, call the doctor.*

Small objects sometimes find their way into children's ears and noses. The child is likely to panic. Calm the child, and keep the child from putting his or her fingers into the ear or nose.

What to Do

1 If the object is loose and you can see it plainly, tip the child's head to see if it will fall out.

2 **If you can't see the object plainly, or if it appears tightly wedged in, leave it alone.** Call the parents or doctor. Don't try to pry the object out—you may just push it in further. Follow the parents' or doctor's instructions carefully.

3 Calm the child.

Stings and Bites

> *If the child has a severe allergic reaction, call the rescue squad.*

Animal or People Bites

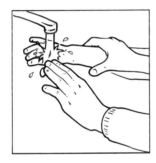

1 Calm the child. Wash the bitten area gently with soap and cool water.

2 Apply an antiseptic to the bandage, and cover the bite securely.

3 Call the parents. If you saw the animal that bit the child, describe it carefully to the parents. Keep the child quiet.

Insect Bites and Stings

1 Calm the child. Wash the bite with soap and cool water. If you see a stinger, remove it.

2 Hold ice wrapped in a cloth to the bite to prevent swelling.

3 Mix a small amount of baking soda with a little water to make a thick paste. Apply the paste to the bite.

4 Mosquito, fly, and spider bites should be washed. Baking soda paste or lotion left by the parents may be applied to stop itching. Ask the parents.

5 Watch for allergic reactions: puffy eyes, sweats, difficulty in breathing.

If the child has a severe allergic reaction, call the rescue squad and get him or her to a hospital emergency room immediately. A severe reaction is marked by difficult breathing and/or vomiting.

Then call the parents.

Stomachache or Pain

If the pain lasts more than one half hour, call the parents. If the child also has a fever, nausea, or vomiting, and you cannot reach the parents quickly, call the doctor.

A child's stomachache may mean nothing more than a need to use the toilet. A child who is upset may also get a stomachache. In this case, your calm concern may help make it go away.

Severe Pain and Pain that Doesn't Stop

1 Do not give the child any food or drink.

2 Call the doctor and then the parents.

3 Give no medication unless you are told to do so.

Be sure to tell the parents about any incidents of stomachaches or pain.

Vomiting

> *Call the parents if the child vomits frequently.*

Infants often spit up while eating, playing, and sleeping. Do not be concerned unless the amount is unusually large, or it happens unusually often.

Vomiting may be a symptom of illness, poisoning, food reaction, or nervousness. Cleaning it up is not fun, but try not to further upset the child by showing your distaste for the job.

What to Do

1 Calm the child and gently clean him or her. If the child is old enough, have the child rinse his or her mouth with cool water and spit it out. Get clean clothing.

2 Wipe the child's hands and face with lukewarm water in order to cool and comfort the child.

3 Give no medication unless specifically told to do so. Do not offer any food or drink until you're sure the child is not going to vomit again. Then offer only small amounts of easy-to-digest foods like jello, crackers, toast, and soda—if allowed. Avoid dairy products.

4 If the child vomits more than once or has a fever or other signs of illness, call the parents.

Otherwise, just tell the parents when they return.

Medical Emergencies

Choking

Infant (under One Year Old)

> *Call the rescue squad.*

If the child is coughing hard, can speak, or is breathing, let the child try to cough the object out.

If the child cannot cough it out or is not breathing, act quickly.

Do not try to remove the object with your fingers. You don't want to push it further into the throat.

> *Do not give the child anything to drink.*

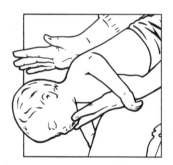

1 With a conscious infant under the age of one, you should use a combination of back blows and chest compressions.

2 Turn the infant onto his or her stomach. Support the infant's lower head and jaw with your hand and straddle the infant's body with your forearm.

3 Rest your forearm on your thigh, and using the heel of your hand, give four forceful blows right between the child's shoulder blades.

4 Now, continuing to support the head, gently turn the baby over and place three fingers over the breast plate right at the nipple line.

5 Lift up the top finger and give four chest compressions.

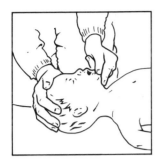

6 If the object fails to dislodge, keep repeating the two sequences over and over.

7 If the infant loses consciousness, open up the child's airway by placing the chin up and forehead back. If you are trained in CPR, use it now. Remember, you must clear the airway.

8 If you are not trained in CPR or cannot clear the airway, take the infant with you and go to the phone and call for help.

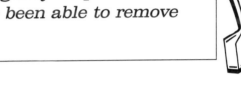

> *Call for emergency help whether or not you've been able to remove the object.*

Child over the Age of One

If the child is coughing hard, can speak, or is breathing, let him or her try to cough the object out. If the child cannot cough it out or is not breathing, act quickly.

> *Do not try to remove the object with your fingers.*
> *You don't want to push it further into the throat.*
> *Do not give the child anything to drink.*

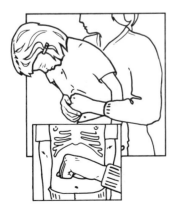

If he or she is unable to speak, cough, or breathe, follow these steps.

1 Stand behind the child, reach around, and place your fist below the rib cage and above the belly button.

2 Cover the fist with your other hand, and push upward and inward to dislodge the object.

3 If the object does not come out, keep doing the maneuver described in steps one and two above (known as the Heimlich maneuver), and have someone call for help.

4 If the child loses consciousness and you know CPR, begin it now. **Remember, the first step is to clear the airway.**

5 If you don't know CPR and you are alone and cannot clear the airway, lay the child down, open the airway by lifting the chin up and the forehead back. Go to the phone and call for help.

Call the doctor even if the object is removed.

> *Call the rescue squad if the object does not pop out.*

Shock

> *Shock can be fatal. Act fast. Always treat for shock when a serious injury occurs.*

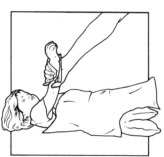

If an injury interrupts the flow of blood to major organs, shock can occur. Shock may appear as very pale or splotchy skin, sweats, rapid or irregular breathing, chills, drooling, dilated pupils, nausea, vomiting, or mental confusion.

Shock may occur as a result of serious injury involving bleeding, broken bones, burns, or poisoning. It is critical to prevent the child from going into shock.

What to Do

1 While you're stopping the bleeding or as soon as possible after treating the injury, have the child lie down.

2 Cover the child with a coat or blanket to maintain normal body temperature. Do not let the child overheat.

3 Put something under the child's feet to raise them slightly higher than head level. Don't do this if it causes breathing difficulty or pain.

4 Do not give the child any drinks or food.

5 Call the doctor or rescue squad. Then call the parents.

Bleeding

A Little Blood: Cuts and Scrapes

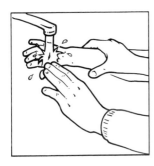

1 Apply light pressure on the wound for about five minutes with a clean bandage, cloth, or towel. Add another cloth on top of the first if necessary.

2 When bleeding stops, gently wash the wound with soap and water. Apply an antiseptic to the bandage. Apply the bandage firmly.

3 If there is glass or a small sharp object in the wound, or if the wound looks deep or wide, call the parents.

A Lot of Blood: A Large Cut that Bleeds A Lot

Call the parents.

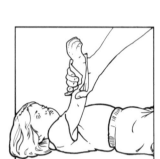

1 Apply pressure on the wound with a clean bandage, cloth, or towel.

2 Raise the arm or leg higher than the heart while applying pressure to the wound.

3 After the bleeding stops, wash the wound gently with soap and water. Apply antiseptic to the bandage. Apply the bandage firmly.

4 Call the parents.

Bleeding Won't Stop

Call the rescue squad.

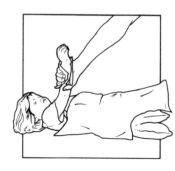

1 Continue to apply pressure to the wound.

2 Keep the limb elevated.

3 Have the child lie down. Raise the child's feet with a pillow or a few books, and cover the child with a blanket or coat to avoid shock.

4 Call the rescue squad first. When the situation is under control, call the parents.

Burns

Minor Burn: No Blister or Small Blister

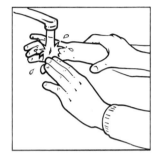

1 Run cold water over the burn for five minutes or until pain stops.

2 Do not apply any medication or bandages.

Severe Burn: Blisters or Broken Skin

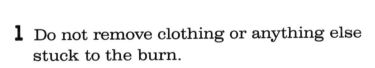

Call the doctor.

Burns Covering a Large Area

Call the rescue squad.

1 Do not remove clothing or anything else stuck to the burn.

2 Cover burned area with clean gauze pads or clean wet cloth.

3 Give the child drinks of cool water.

4 Cover the child with a coat or blanket to prevent shock.

5 After calling for help (doctor or rescue squad), call the parents.

Electrical Burn

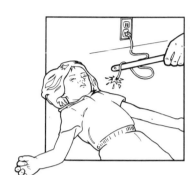

1 Be sure your hands are dry. Use a nonconductive stick, like a broom handle, to lift the electrical wire away from the child. Do not use anything metal to separate the electrical wire from the child. Do not touch the wire directly.

2 Call the rescue squad immediately.

3 Cover the burn with a clean gauze pad or clean cloth.

4 If you can, elevate the burned part. Cover the child with a coat or blanket to prevent shock.

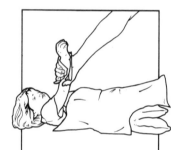

5 Call the parents while you wait for the rescue squad.

Chemical Burn

1 Flush the burned area with cool water for five full minutes. If the area is large, put the child in a cool shower.

2 Cover the burn with a clean gauze pad or clean cloth.

3 Cover the child with a coat or blanket to prevent shock.

4 Call rescue squad. Then call the parents.

Difficulty Breathing

Begin artificial respiration immediately.

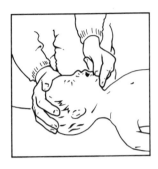

1 Clear mouth of loose gum or food.

2 If airway is blocked, follow these instructions.
For an infant: See instructions for infants, pages 94–5.
For an older child: See instructions for older child, pages 95–6.

3 Help the child breathe.

For an Infant:

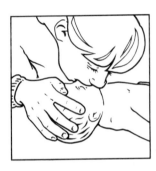

1 Open the airway by tilting the forehead back and lifting the chin up.

2 Cover the infant's mouth and nose with your mouth.

3 Breathe into the child once every three seconds using puffs of air in your cheeks.

Call the rescue squad.

For an Older Child:

1 Open the airway by tilting the forehead back and lifting the chin up.

2 Pinch the child's nostrils closed and cover the child's mouth with your mouth.

3 Give two quick gentle breaths into the mouth of the child. Then one breath every 3–5 seconds.

4 See if the chest is rising and falling on its own. If not, try to clear the airway again—and repeat all the steps.

> *If the child is not breathing,*
> *continue until help arrives.*

Remember, you are doing all you can to save the life of this child. You must stay calm and in control. You must do the best you can to keep this child alive until help arrives. You will be surprised at how much you know and how much you can do in this emergency. Do not let your own fear, panic, or insecurity stand in the way of what you *must* and *can* do. As you breathe with this child, imagine you are breathing life and health into the child, and strength and confidence into yourself. Be strong and have faith. It is a wonderful thing to save a life.

Poisoning

> *Call poison control.*

1 Try to determine what was swallowed.

2 Call the poison control center or the doctor. Have paper and pencil ready to write down instructions. Calmly tell them:

  • The address and phone number where you are.

  • What was swallowed and how much.

  • The age of the child.

  • "I'm the babysitter."

Follow their instructions. Do not give any medication or drinks without specific instructions to do so.

Symptoms of Poisoning

Vomiting, burns on face and mouth, sudden change in behavior, thirst, sweats, stains and odors on clothing, difficulty breathing, convulsions, and unconsciousness are symptoms of poisoning.

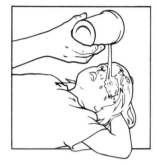

Poison in the Eye or on the Skin

1 Rinse with lukewarm water. Be careful not to get water into nose or mouth.

2 Call the doctor, then call the parents.

Poisonous Fumes

> *Call the doctor.*

1 Open windows or take child into fresh air immediately.

2 Call the doctor.

After you've taken appropriate action, call the parents. If you're instructed to go to a hospital, carefully take the poisonous substance with you so the doctors can test it.

List of Common Household Poisons

Alcohol
Ammonia
Antifreeze
Antihistamines (cold medicines)
Aspirin (in large quantities)
Birth control pills and creams
Bleach
Bug spray

Cleaners
Perfume and cologne
Deodorant, personal and room
Detergents
Drain cleaner
Fabric softener
Fingernail polish and remover
Gasoline
Hair care products

Iodine
Paints and markers
Paint remover/thinner
Kerosene
Lighter fluid
Lye
Mothballs
Pain killers

Polish and wax
Suntan lotion
Toiletries
Tranquilizers
Turpentine
Weed killer
Wide variety of plants

Convulsions

During a convulsion, the child may stiffen, fall to the ground, twitch, froth at the mouth, have his or her eyes roll upward, urinate or deficate, or lose consciousness. While a convulsion may look frightening, it is usually not dangerous.

What to Do

1 Your job is to be sure the child does not hurt himself/herself. If possible, place the child on the carpet or floor away from furniture and breakables.

2 Loosen the child's clothing, especially around the neck.

> *Be sure the child is breathing. If not, begin artificial respiration. See page 101 of this handbook.*

3 Do not try to restrain the child. Do not give the child anything to drink during the convulsion. Do not put anything between the child's teeth. The child will *not* swallow his or her tongue.

4 Observe the child's behavior. Note what parts of the body twitch or shake. If the child is drooling, roll the child onto his or her side to prevent choking.

5 Call the doctor.

When the convulsion stops, gently put the child in bed. Call the parents.

After a convulsion, a child will most likely be very scared, confused, and possibly embarrassed. Now that the child is safe, it is time to attend to these feelings. In fact, you'll probably *both* need to calm down. As you attend to the child with gentle, soothing words, you'll hopefully find yourself relaxing a little as well. You've both shared a difficult time.

Unconsciousness

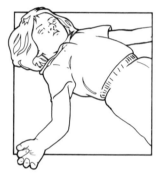

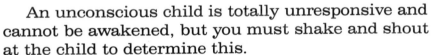

Call the rescue squad.

An unconscious child is totally unresponsive and cannot be awakened, but you must shake and shout at the child to determine this.

1 Call the rescue squad, and follow their directions.

2 Open the airway by tilting the forehead back and chin up.

3 If the child is not breathing and you know CPR, begin it now.

If you do not know CPR and the child is not breathing, begin artificial respiration. See page 101 of this manual.

You are working to save a life, and there isn't much time. You must be strong and brave and do what you can to help this child breathe.

> *Get emergency help first.*

Call the parents while you're waiting for help to arrive.

Broken Bones

> *Call the doctor.*

Do not move the child if there is any chance a bone is broken.

1 Cover the child with a coat or blanket. Call the doctor, then call the parents.

2 If you're outside, try to get a nearby adult or older child to call an ambulance so you can remain with the child.

Stay with the injured child until help arrives. Then call the parents. Serious injuries can result from improperly moving a child with broken bones. If the child is in a particularly dangerous location—be sure to tell the ambulance attendants.

Something in the Eye

Small Objects in the Eye

1 The child's tears may wash the object out.

2 If not, get a clean cloth. Pull back the eyelid. Use the corner of the cloth to pick out the object. Never use your finger or a hard instrument.

When the Object Is Stuck into the Eye

Call the rescue squad.

1 Don't touch it, and don't let the child touch it.

2 Cover the eye loosely with gauze.

3 Get the child to the doctor or the hospital immediately. Call the rescue squad or a neighbor.

4 Then call the parents.

Cuts to the Eye

Call the doctor, and follow instructions.

1 Treat the eyelid and the area around the eye only. Wash gently with water and cover with small bandage if needed. Cover the eye loosely with gauze.

2 Any injury to the eye itself requires a doctor. Don't touch it.

3 Call the doctor or the rescue squad. Then call the parents.

Chemicals in the Eye

> *Call the rescue squad.*

1 Flush the eye with water for a full five minutes under the faucet or by pouring water from a glass or cup. Try not to let water get into the other eye, nose, or mouth.

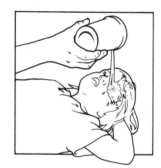

2 Cover the eye loosely with clean gauze.

3 Call the rescue squad. Then call the parents.

Swallowing Something Wrong

If the object is small enough to be swallowed without choking, the child is not in any danger—unless the object is poisonous or sharp or gets lodged in the throat and blocks the airway.

> *If poisonous, see pages 102–3 of this manual and call poison control.*
>
> *If the child is choking, see pages 94–6 of this manual.*
>
> *If the child swallowed a sharp object, call the rescue squad and then the parents.*

Household Emergencies

Fire

> *Call the fire department!*
>
> *Get the children!*
>
> *Get out of the house!*

1 If there is smoke in the house, stay close to the floor to prevent smoke inhalation while you are trying to get out. Use wet cloths to cover faces; it makes it easier to breathe.

2 Test doors for heat before opening. If the door is cool, open it as little as possible to get out.

If the door is hot, do not open. Try another exit. Close the door behind you. If you must wait for rescue, wait near a window and open the window just slightly for air. Too much air helps fire spread. Hang clothing or other object out the window to help rescuers locate you.

Clothes on Fire

1 Don't let the child run.

2 Put the child on the floor, and roll him or her over and over slowly.

Smother burning clothes with a blanket, coat, or other item made with heavy fabric, like a small throw rug.

Don't worry about saving anything except the children and yourself. GO!

See "Burns," pages 99–100.

Kitchens and Grease Fires

Grease fires cannot be put out with water.

1 Be sure children are safe.

2 Cover burning pot with lid or another pot.

 If handy, smother flames with baking soda or salt.

3 If you can't put the fire out quickly...GET THE CHILDREN OUT.

Call the fire department from a neighbor's phone.

Prowler

If you see someone lurking outside the house who seems suspicious and has no reason for being there, take these steps:

Stay inside.

Be sure all doors are locked.

Call the police.

Calmly tell the police:

1 The address and telephone number of the house and the family name.

2 "I'm the babysitter."

3 Describe what you saw or heard. Give as much detail as possible about the appearance of the prowler, his or her movements and actions. If you see the prowler leave, note the direction in which the prowler goes. Try to write down the license plate of the prowler's car.

> *Be sure not to alarm the children.*

Remember, normal outside and house noises often seem louder when you're alone babysitting. But if the noise doesn't seem normal, call the police.

Be sure to tell the parents what happened. They'll be glad to know you're protecting their child.

Power Failure

> *Be calm.*
>
> *If it's daytime, you can get by without electricity.*

If it's nighttime:

1 Reassure the child(ren).

2 Locate the flashlight and/or candles and matches. If you're using candles, be sure they're safely out of the child's reach.

3 Don't allow roughhousing in the dark.

Call the electric company. You may want to call the parents just to let them know what's happening. Try not to open the refrigerator and freezer any more than necessary. If you need to warm a baby bottle, run it under hot tap water. Test it for temperature before giving it to the infant.

If You Smell Gas

> *Keep the child close to you.*
>
> *Don't light any matches.*
>
> *Don't turn any light switches on or off.*

1 Check the stove to see if burners are off.

2 If you can't immediately find the source of the leak . . . *or* . . . If the smell is very strong,

3 Get out of the house.

4 Go to a neighbor's house or to the apartment building manager. Ask an adult to try to locate the source of the leak, turn it off, and open the windows.

5 If the source of the leak is found and eliminated, go outside or stay near an open window until the smell is gone.

When in doubt, leave. Call the gas company, then call the parents. Gas fumes can be serious.

If a Water Pipe Breaks

Once in a while, a water pipe breaks in the home. First, be sure the child is in a safe, dry area away from the water. Be careful of any electrical wires or appliances in the area where water is leaking. Don't touch any wires. These wires, when in contact with water, can cause severe electrical shock.

Call the parents. If you can't reach them, and there is more than a small leak, call the plumber or the building manager. If you can do it safely, put some towels just beyond where the water is spreading to keep the water contained in a limited area. If you can move any items that might get damaged by the water, do so. But remember not to take any chances, the child is your main responsibility.

Water Shut-Off Valve

Parents should have written the location of the main water shut off on your forms. If it is safe for you and the child, turn this valve off. **Do not leave the child unattended or place him or her in any danger in order to do this.**

For water main breaks that occur outside, call the city water department.

Storms and Tornadoes

Especially in spring, summer, and fall, thunderstorms and tornadoes may occur. Be alert to sudden changes in the weather. Listen for sirens. Turn on a battery-operated radio and follow any weather-related instructions.

1 Keep the child inside.

2 Close windows and doors as much as necessary to keep rain out.

3 Locate flashlights and batteries, candles, and

matches. Be sure to keep candles and matches out of the reach of the child.

4 A tornado watch means weather conditions are right for the formation of tornadoes. Listen carefully to your battery powered radio.

5 A tornado warning means an actual tornado has been sighted. Take the children, flashlights/candles, and radio to a safe location in the basement or an inside hallway—away from doors, windows, bookshelves, and heavy furniture that could fall and cause injury. Stay in the safe place until the tornado warning has been officially cancelled.

If possible, call the parents and tell them about the severe weather conditions. They may want to return home or give you specific instructions for safety. Stay calm. Make up stories with the kids. Sing songs.

If You Get Sick

If you become ill or injured, call a nearby relative, friend, or neighbor to relieve you. Call the parents and tell them who is coming and why. Never leave children unattended.

If you can't find a suitable person to relieve you, call the parents and stay with the child until they return.

Nuisance Calls

Repeated wrong numbers, frightening calls, annoying calls, and obscene calls are all legitimate reasons for concern.

> *Don't talk to the caller. Hang up.*

Even if it seems like a friendly call, don't tell anyone that you are the babysitter and are alone. Don't tell them that the parents aren't home or where they are. Say something like: "I'm sorry, they're not available to come to the phone right now, but can they call you back soon? Would you like to leave a message?

> *If you sense an immediate threat, call the police.*
> *Be sure all doors are locked. Stay inside.*

If you're uneasy, call a member of your family to come and stay with you. Or call the parents—they may decide to come home. Don't take unnecessary chances. And try not to alarm the child.

If Something Breaks or Spills

Don't get upset. It happens. If the child caused the accident, try not to get angry. The child is probably frightened and upset enough already.

Things that Go Crash

1 Remove the child to a safe place. An older child may want to help clean up. Just be sure not to let the child handle broken glass.

2 If the broken item is electrical, unplug it.

3 Be sure everyone is wearing shoes.

4 Clean up as much as possible, putting dangerous pieces safely out of the way. Save broken pieces that may be able to be repaired.

5 Tell the parents what happened when they return. Most parents don't appreciate finding surprises.

Things that Spill

1 Soak up spills immediately by placing an absorbent material on top of the spill and pressing down. Continue with fresh paper towel or napkin until no more food or liquid is absorbed. Try not to rub the spill into the carpet or fabric.

2 Cold water will rinse most food spills out of clothes.

3 Do not use any cleaning products on carpet or furniture without specific instructions to do so.

4 If you're concerned about stains, call the parents for instructions. Most parents prefer a telephone call to a permanent grape juice stain on their sofa.

Medical Treatment Consent Form

I (we) authorize the provision of necessary and appropriate medical care for my (our) minor child (children), including x-ray, anesthetic, medical and surgical diagnosis and treatment, and hospitalization under the supervision of a physician or surgeon licensed to practice medicine in the State of _____. I (we) assume full financial responsibility for medical and surgical care provided.

Please contact me (us) as soon as possible after my child(ren) is brought in for treatment.

This consent remains valid and in effect for twelve (12) months from the date of signature unless cancelled or superceded.

child	birthdate	blood type	allergies

signature: _____   date: _____

signature: _____   date: _____

Preferred hospital

name: _____

address: _____   phone: _____

Preferred physicians:

pediatrician: _____   phone: _____

dentist: _____   phone: _____

other: _____   phone: _____

Additional Resources

The following videotapes provide useful additional information on baby sitting, child care, and emergency first aid. They are available from Super Sitters, Inc., P.O. Box 218, Mequon, Wisconsin 53092; telephone number (414) 242-2411.

Super Sitter Basics.   Jay Litvin and Dr. Lee Salk, Super Sitters, Inc., Mequon, Wisconsin. A 30-minute VHS video teaching the basics of safe, compassionate sitting of infants, toddlers, and older children.

Baby Alive!   Featuring Phylicia Rashad, Action Film and Video, Inc., New York, N.Y. A 60-minute video, approved by the American Academy of Pediatrics, presenting a step-by-step guide for prevention and treatment of life-threatening situations facing children from birth to 5 years old.

How to Save Your Child or Baby When Every Second Counts.   Producer, Pacific Stat Systems, Los Angeles, Cal., 1988. CPR and Heimlich maneuver for infants and children.

Emergency Action: The life saving first aid video for the whole family.   Dr. Stanley Zydio, produced by ActiVideo, Chicago, Ill., 1988. A 30-minute VHS video on what to do until the ambulance arrives when dealing with emergencies such as choking, poisoning, fire, deep cuts, burns, smoke inhalation, and frostbite.